PEDRO, THE GREAT PRETENDER

Miguel de Cervantes

PEDRO, THE GREAT PRETENDER

in a new version by Philip Osment

after literal translations by Simon Masterton
and Jack Sage / Kathleen Mountjoy

OBERON BOOKS
LONDON

The Royal Shakespeare Company

The Royal Shakespeare Company is one of the world's best known theatre ensembles, which aims to create outstanding theatre relevant to our times. The RSC is at the leading edge of classical theatre, with an international reputation for artistic excellence, accessibility and high quality live performance.

The Spanish Golden Age celebrates one of the most dynamic, energetic and stylish periods of world drama that is, astonishingly, hardly known to any of us. The four neglected plays from 17th century Spain which the RSC chose to present dramatised our fascination with the themes of seduction, honour and revenge.

The season is unique in a number of ways. It is the first time that an ensemble of British actors has come together over a period of time to bring these plays to life. It is a new venture for the RSC and also importantly for many of our audiences who have not had the opportunity to see the plays before.

The RSC performs throughout the year at our home in Stratford-upon-Avon and that work is complemented by a presence in other areas of the UK. We play regularly in London and at an annual residency in Newcastle upon Tyne. In addition, our mobile auditorium tour sets up in community centres, sports halls and schools in areas throughout the UK with little access to professional theatre.

While the UK is the home of our Company, our audiences are global. We regularly play to theatregoers in other parts of Europe, across the United States, the Americas, Asia and Australasia and we are proud of our relationships with partnering organisations throughout the world.

The RSC is at heart an ensemble Company. The continuation of this great tradition informs the work of all members of the Company. Directors, actors, dramatists and theatre practitioners all collaborate in the creation of the RSC's distinctive and unmistakable approach to theatre.

 **The Royal Shakespeare Company**

Patron
Her Majesty The Queen
President
His Royal Highness The Prince of Wales
Deputy President
Sir Geoffrey Cass MA CIMgt

Artistic Director
Michael Boyd
Executive Director
Vikki Heywood

Board
Sir Christopher Bland *(Chairman)*
Lady Sainsbury of Turville *(Deputy Chairman)*
Prof Jonathan Bate FBA
Neil W Benson OBE
Jane Drabble OBE
Janet M Gaymer CBE
Sara Harrity MBE
Michael Hoffman
Laurence Isaacson CBE
Nicholas Lovegrove
Dana G Mead
Andrew Seth
A K Wilson MA

The Royal Shakespeare Company is incorporated under Royal
Charter and is a registered charity, number 212481.

A PARTNERSHIP WITH THE RSC

The RSC relies on the active involvement and the direct charitable support of our audience members for contributions towards our work. Members of our audience also assist by introducing us to companies, foundations and other organisations with which they have an involvement – and help us demonstrate that in return for either philanthropic or sponsorship support, we can deliver benefit to audiences, local communities, school groups and all those who are given enhanced access to our work through private sector support.

RSC PATRONS AND SHAKESPEARE'S CIRCLE

Personal contributions from RSC Patrons provide essential financial support for our artists, educationalists and their students, young writers and audience members that require special access services.

For more information, please contact the Development Department on **01789 272 283**.

CORPORATE PARTNERSHIPS

The RSC has a global reputation, undertaking more international touring each year than any other UK arts organisation. Our profile is high; our core values of artistic excellence and outstanding performance can be aligned with commercial values and objectives.

Our extensive range of productions and outreach and education programmes help ensure that we identify the best opportunity to deliver your particular business objectives. A prestigious programme of corporate hospitality and membership packages is also available.

For more information, please contact the Development Department on **01789 272 283**.

For detailed information about opportunities to support the work of the RSC, visit **www.rsc.org.uk/support**

This production of *Pedro, the Great Pretender* was first performed by the Royal Shakespeare Company in the Swan Theatre, Stratford-upon-Avon, on 1 September 2004.

The original cast was as follows:

William Buckhurst	Pascual
	Diego-Fly-The-Coop
James Chalmers	Diego Tarugo
	Director
Joseph Chance	Hornachuelos
	Llorente
	Farmer
Claire Cox	Belica
Julius D'Silva	Martín Crespo
	Singer
Rebecca Johnson	The Queen
Katherine Kelly	Benita
Melanie MacHugh	Marina Sánchez
Joseph Millson	The King
Vinta Morgan	Roque
	Gil The Carder
	Third Player
Emma Pallant	Clemencia (Clemency)
Oscar Pearce	Lagartija
	Silerio
John Ramm	Pedro the Great Pretender
Matt Ryan	A Blind Man
	Second Player
Peter Sproule	Marcelo
John Stahl	Maldonado
Simon Trinder	Clemente
	Attendant
Joanna Van Kampen	Inés
John Wark	Sancho Macho
	First Player
	Singer
Oliver Williams	Redondo
	Master

All other parts played by members of the Company

Directed by	Mike Alfreds
New translation by	Philip Osment
Literal translators	Simon Masterton
	Jack Sage / Kathleen Mountjoy
Designed by	Rae Smith
Season stage designed by	Es Devlin
Lighting designed by	Ben Ormerod
Music composed by	Ilona Sekacz
Sound designed by	Mike Compton
Movement by	Leah Hausman
Assistant Director	Chris White
Music Director	Michael Tubbs
Company voice work by	Jeannette Nelson
Casting Director	John Cannon CDG
Costume Supervisor	Johanna Coe
Production Manager	Pete Griffin
Company Manager	Jondon
Stage Manager	Paul Sawtell
Deputy Stage Manager	Jenny Grand
Assistant Stage Manager	Ruth Taylor

Contents

First published in 2004 by Oberon Books Ltd
(incorporating Absolute Classics)
521 Caledonian Road, London N7 9RH
Tel: 020 7607 3637 / Fax: 020 7607 3629

e-mail: oberon.books@btinternet.com
www.oberonbooks.com

The following translation was correct at the time of going to press,
but may differ from the play as performed.

A catalogue record for this book is available from the British
Library.

ISBN: 1 84002 443 7

Cover design: Ann-marie Comarsh, RSC Graphics

Illustration by Cristina Rodero / agence VU

Printed in Great Britain by Antony Rowe Ltd, Chippenham.

Characters (in order of speaking)

CLEMENTE, a shepherd

PEDRO THE GREAT PRETENDER

BENITA, a shepherdess

CLEMENCIA (Clemency), a shepherdess

DIEGO TARUGO, an alderman

MARTÍN CRESPO, Mayor and father to CLEMENCIA

SANCHO MACHO, an alderman

LAGARTIJA, a peasant farmer

HORNACHUELOS, a peasant farmer

REDONDO, a scribe

PASCUAL, a shepherd

ROQUE, a sexton

MALDONADO, The Gypsy Chief

INÉS, a gypsy girl

BELICA (Belilla/Isabél), a gypsy girl

MARINA SÁNCHEZ, a widow and farmer

LLORENTE, her squire.

DIEGO-FLY-THE-COOP, a farm worker, nephew to the
MAYOR

GIL THE CARDER, a farm worker*

MASTER OF THE REVELS

A BLIND MAN

---

* A character referred to in the Spanish text who appears in the RSC production.

THE KING

SILERIO, a servant to the King

THE QUEEN

GENTLEMAN*

MARCELO, an old nobleman

FARMER with two hens

PLAYERS, and

DIRECTOR of the troupe

PEASANTS, GYPSY DANCERS, MUSICIANS
and SINGERS

*   In the RSC production he is the Queen's attendant.

ACT ONE

Enter PEDRO THE GREAT PRETENDER dressed as a young farmhand with CLEMENTE as a shepherd.

CLEMENTE: Ingenious Pedro, between us two
      exists a friendship that won't die;
      there is a wiliness in you,
      on which I'm sure I can rely;
      the whole world knows this to be true!

      Your wit and our friendly relations,
      how high they rank in my estimation!
      And so on them I place my trust –
      as in my present state I must –
      to be my succour and salvation.

      What have I done to affront her,
      your master's daughter Clemency?
      I'd call her Merciless and confront her,
      but that, always, she flies from me
      as the stag flies from the hunter.

      Nature has made her supreme,
      more lovely than your wildest dream,
      so I'm in this pitiful state
      and my suffering won't abate –
      just like her beauty, it's extreme!

      Just when I thought that all my trying
      had made her see my love was true –
      all that longing, all that sighing –
      someone came, I don't know who,
      and changed my lamb into a lion.

      Nor do I know what sort of lies
      have turned the meekness in her eyes
      to anger; nor why Cupid's dart

        is sent to pierce my suffering heart;
        nor why I'm left to agonise.

PEDRO: Stop babbling! Tell me directly
        what you want.
CLEMENTE: Pedro, my brother
        I want you to set me free
        by some wise counsel or other;
        a shrewd man like you has the key.

PEDRO: Have your amorous desires
        gone beyond talking hearts and flowers?
        Have you yet touched on the spot –
        where Love always aims his shot –
        the place to which he aspires?

CLEMENTE: I'm only a shepherd you know
        so can you please speak with less art?
        I can't grasp it when you talk so.
PEDRO: I'm asking when playing your part
        are you high-flown or do you aim low?

CLEMENTE: What an assumption you've made!
        Clemente does not masquerade!
        How dare you suggest it's an act!
PEDRO: *(Aside.)* For oafs like this best stick to fact
        a spade must always be a spade.

        Did ever you and Clemency meet,
        alone or in some private place,
        when she let you be indiscreet
        and do something we might call base
        which puts your conscience in retreat?

CLEMENTE: Pedro, may the heavens strike me down,
        may I be swallowed by the ground,
        may I be smothered by the air
        if in the love that I bear
        her, impropriety be found.

Her father's wealthy circumstances
mean that he looks down on me
I'm not his equal so my chances
don't look good with Clemency –
it's someone richer that he fancies.

This is understandable, for
a woman's heart's not going to soar
borne aloft solely on love;
no, it's how much gold she'll have
in her possession that matters more.

And besides all that, my Clemency
does not love me in return,
because of some trumped up story
that she's been told, which I can't learn,
that's made her hide herself from me.

If Pedro cannot bring us peace
making this quarrelling cease
then I'll have to throw my hand in.
PEDRO: Either I lack understanding
or I'll soon bring you some release.

If, as in my expectation,
my master becomes mayor today,
then it's my prognostication
that fate's not brought you here in vain
to undertake this conversation.

I shall hand you easily
the treasure that your poverty
has denied you until now.
Before that there will be, I vow,
a betrothal and a dowry.

Meanwhile turn you eyes, for there
you may see the loving ties
that bind you – Cupid's snare!

It's for her that Phoebus sighs
as he shines on her fair hair.

In Clemencia's lovely tresses
how lasciviously Love expresses
admiration, seeing himself there,
his reflection in those locks where
he cavorts like a Narcissus.

With her comes a second light
her cousin Benita like a star
beside the sun, wishing she might
not be eclipsed, stay on a par,
send out radiance just as bright.

Clemente, hear now what I say:
if Clemencia should come this way
bow to her; I'll do the same
to Benita, blessed by name,
whom I'll respectfully waylay.

The things your skilful tongue will swear
must make her forget she's mad;
there's not a woman anywhere –
here's a truth that's ironclad –
who isn't thrilled when she's called fair.

Spread this coinage with open hand
let your voice not cease to sound
praises to her, and you'll see,
set in motion inexorably,
fickle fortune's wheel turn round.

*Enter CLEMENCIA and BENITA, shepherdesses, with their
pitchers as if on their way to the well.*

BENITA: Clemencia, why turn your back?
CLEMENCIA: Why I turn, Benita? Why?
Because I'd rather not cross tracks

with him who takes my health away:
It's his fault that I'm on the rack.

He's someone I can't bear to see;
he has insolence in plenty;
unlike his name, he's most unkind.

BENITA: Then I know who you have in mind,
I'd wager that his name's Clemente!

CLEMENTE: It's as if, when I am near,
you see a ghost, my shepherdess,
or a basilisk who appears
out of nowhere whose dreadfulness,
paralyses you with fear.

CLEMENCIA: You're all talk and nothing more,
fawning, flattering – so cocksure,
even though you have no reason;
in your lies the truth is found;
in truth you're false right to the core.

But above all what's false is
what you seem to think I'd do,
without grounds for the prognosis,
if another came to woo:
'I'd be yours and no-one else's?'

This is what you told Jacinta
to put it quite succinctly,
and showed her the belt I gave you;
it was scarlet, so's your face too;
it betrays the truth distinctly.

CLEMENTE: Clemencia, if anything I've spoken
has not aimed to serve you faithfully,
may I be brought down from the greatest fortune
to languish in a pit of bleak despair;
if my tongue has ever failed to raise you
way beyond the circle of the moon,

may I be silenced by the heavens above,
when next I come to make complaints of love.

[If that was what I showed her, my lack of faith
should bring me condemnation at my death
by all the laws of love, by which I'd hoped
that my good faith was going to bring salvation;
if that was what I told her, Cupid needs
no cooling arrows of lead in his quiver,
unless they're aimed at you, as you're all ice,
but golden ones for me, as I'm all fire.]*

PEDRO: Clemencia, your father's close
    carrying his mayoral rod.
CLEMENCIA: He didn't get that on the nod,
    he paid for it through the nose.

    Brother, Clement, I say adieu –
CLEMENTE: How are things between us two?
CLEMENCIA: Good.
    Let's go, Benita, I think we should.
BENITA: Clemencia I agree with you.

    They exit.

PEDRO: So, Clemente, it's time you went!
    Just you leave it all to me,
    I'll handle things effectively.
CLEMENTE: God bless you!
PEDRO: And make you content.

*Enter MARTÍN CRESPO the Mayor, Clemencia's father, with
SANCHO MACHO and DIEGO TARUGO, aldermen.*

TARUGO: We're so pleased Crespo at your succession
    though it's a shame your rod is not embossed.
    A bit of gold makes such a good impression.

---

*   Text inside square brackets denotes that it was cut from the RSC production.

CRESPO: Diego Tarugo, what this rod has cost,
    is something that God alone can know,
    as do the cattle, cocks and wines I've lost.

    Gaining office takes a heavy toll –
    it's heavier than you think it's going to be.
SANCHO: A candidacy brings much care and woe,

    I'd only wish it on an enemy;
    let him shell out for such a rod as this.
CRESPO: Now it's your friend who's shelled out, as you see.

SANCHO: You'll rule so well with this rod of office,
    it won't be bent by pleas or gifts in kind.
CRESPO: On my life I swear I won't be so remiss!

    If a woman's my informer, I'll be blind;
    if some gent's the plaintiff then I'll be deaf mute;
    I'll be the harshest judge you'll ever find.

TARUGO: Your time will be a time, there's no dispute,
    like Solomon's with sentences as wise:
    he used sharp steel to cleave a child in two.

CRESPO: Take heed that Crespo hereby testifies,
    he'll try to stick to what is legal and right,
    in no decree will there be compromise.

SANCHO: May this mean that our future will be bright.
    Adieu.
CRESPO: Sancho Macho, on Fortune's wheel,
    may you stay at the very highest height!

TARUGO: May neither love nor fear affect your zeal
    for passing judgement with the swiftest rigour;
    on slowness blame is quick to set its seal.
    Adieu.
CRESPO: Farewell cousin, most worthy figure!

Exeunt SANCHO MACHO and DIEGO TARUGO.

Pedro, you stand listening here,
and though I've had this big success,
no 'Well done, Master!' do I hear.
I am mayor but nonetheless,
it will be for nothing I fear,

if I don't get your tuition
to help me judge with precision.
Do me this favour, use your art;
you have more wisdom to impart
than any priest or physician.

PEDRO: In this opinion you're correct,
judging by what I'll do for you;
for I will be the architect
of a simple little scheme to
earn you renown and much respect.

Socrates will barely reach you
and famed Athens will beseech you,
silencing its learned laws,
kings approach you on all fours;
there'll be nothing schools can teach you.

In your hood I'm going to place –
this will make the whole world rapt –
two dozen sentences which embrace
every judgement; they'll be apt
for every trial and civil case.

The first one that comes to hand
will answer every demand,
nothing left to quarrel about.
CRESPO: From now you'll be, without a doubt,
my brother, not my serving-man.

[Come now, Pedro, show me the way,
and tell me what I need to do
to achieve the things you say.

PEDRO: I'll show you more, I promise you.
CRESPO: You be master, I'll obey.]

Exeunt the MAYOR and PEDRO.
Enter SANCHO MACHO and TARUGO.

SANCHO: Look, Tarugo, it's my guess,
  that though I heard you say, 'Bravo'
  to Crespo on his success,
  really you were thinking, 'Oh no!',
  but kept that thought close to your chest.

  It's a shame, I can't but feel,
  that our town's got this imbecile;
  you'll not find a more foolish man
  from Greece to the Netherlands
  or from Egypt to Castile.

TARUGO: Today's events are going to show
  what sort of mayor he's going to be,
  so good Alderman Sancho,
  I'm simply going to wait and see
  how things at his first hearing go.

  And since it must be starting soon
  I think it would be opportune
  to stay and listen.
SANCHO: I agree,
  although as far as I can see,
  he's going to look like a buffoon.

Enter LAGARTIJA and HORNACHUELOS, peasants.

HORNACHUELOS: Please Sirs, can we learn from you
  if the mayor's at home today?
TARUGO: We are waiting for him too.
LAGARTIJA: That's a sign he'll come this way.
SANCHO: Here he is, which proves that true.

Enter the MAYOR and REDONDO, the clerk, with PEDRO.

CRESPO: Oh most valiant aldermen!

REDONDO: Most worthy Sirs, please take a seat.

CRESPO: No ceremony, gentlemen!

TARUGO: Your courtesy may well exceed
   that of the most polite of men.

CRESPO: Let the clerk be seated here,
   and at my left and at my right hand,
   let the aldermen appear,
   and you, Pedro, you should stand
   at my back.

PEDRO: That's very clear.

   Here in your hood now you have got
   all the sentences you need to
   judge every case no matter what,
   but I urge you, pay no heed to
   whether they're pertinent or not.

   And if none of them suffices
   just turn and ask what my advice is;
   I'll counsel you in such a way,
   to extricate you come what may,
   never mind how great the crisis.

REDONDO: Can we help you, Sirs?

LAGARTIJA: Indeed you can.

REDONDO: Then speak, the man you see here is the mayor,
   and from him you'll get justice fair and square.

CRESPO: May God forgive what I'm about to say,
   and may it not be seen as arrogance:
   when I judge I'm going to be severer
   than Roman senators in hysteria.

REDONDO: In history, Worship.

CRESPO: It makes no odds.
   Be brief and hasty when you state your case:
   when my soul hears your words, I'll dissect 'em,
   then I'll pass a sentence with my rectum.

REDONDO: With rectitude, Worship?

CRESPO: It makes no odds.

HORNACHUELOS: Lagartija lent me three sovereigns,
   I gave back two, which leaves one to be paid,
   and he maintains that I still owe him four.
   That's the case, your Briefness, and I'm done.

CRESPO: Good Lagartija now, is this the truth?

LAGARTIJA: True. However on my account I find,
   that either I'm an ass or Hornachuelos
   does owe me four.

CRESPO: A fascinating case!

LAGARTIJA: That's the sum of our dispute and I'll concuss
   with any sentence that the mayor shall give.

REDONDO: Concuss and not concur, it makes no odds.

CRESPO: What have you to say now, Hornachuelos?

HORNACHUELOS: There's nothing more to say, I'll convalesce
   with Señor Crespo.

REDONDO: Oh my giddy aunt!
   It's acquiesce!

CRESPO: Let him convalesce,
   what's it to you, Redondo?

REDONDO: To me? Nothing!

CRESPO: Pedro, take a sentence from this hood,
   my friend, the first one that comes to your hand.

REDONDO: Before the case is tried there's to be sentence?

CRESPO: Now we're going to see who's top dog.

PEDRO: Read the sentence and then Bob's your uncle!

REDONDO: 'In the case of L versus P" –

PEDRO: Litigate and Piggot – a famous case!

REDONDO: Alright as I was saying, 'In the case
   of Mister Litigate v Mister Piggot,
   as trial judge I duly pronounce sentence
   according to the laws of sheep slaughter
   and condemn said Piggot's boar to death
   for having killed a creature belonging

to said Litigate –' I just can't see
what the heck this stuff about a pig
and nonsense about Litigates and Piggots
has got to do with these two men's dispute.

CRESPO: Redondo is quite right about this, Pedro,
if you put in your hand and take another;
maybe the one you find will be more use.

PEDRO: I, your assessor, now make bold to pass
a sentence that I think you might find apt.

LAGARTIJA: And I will if it buys me a new donkey.

SANCHO: Our assessor really is extraordinary!

HORNACHUELOS: Pass sentence well and good.

CRESPO: Yes, go on Pedro
I'm banking on your wit to save my name.

PEDRO: First let Hornachuelos do the banking
by giving twelve sovereigns to me.

HORNACHUELOS: The case only concerns half that amount!

PEDRO: The truth goes thus: that from good Lagartija
you borrowed three double sov'reigns in fact.
The two coins you returned were only singles;
and so on the account remain four sovereigns
and not as you yourself claim, merely one.

LAGARTIJA: That's just how it is, no word of a lie!

HORNACHUELOS: You've got me bang to rights I can't deny.
I'll pay you twelve and him the four I owe him.

REDONDO: (*Aside.*) Let Cato and Justinian kiss my arse now!
Pedro you really are a great Pretender!
For such skill shows your name is well-deserved.

HORNACHUELOS: I'll go get the cash, I'm put to shame.

LAGARTIJA: And I'm content because I overcame.

*Enter CLEMENTE and CLEMENCIA as shepherd and
shepherdess with faces covered.*

CLEMENTE: Do you permit us to speak incognito
to a court so just and so upright?

CRESPO: Speak tied up in a sack and I won't veto,
      I sit and use my hearing not my sight.

CLEMENTE: The centuries famed for being golden
      in olden times which justly earned the name,
      are seen again in the highest extreme
      in these our times where justice reigns supreme.

      To see a Crespo mayor –
CRESPO: God keep you well
      but leave these condiments, and tell me straight –
REDONDO: Compliments, you mean!
CRESPO: Will you please tell
      what you intend? Be brief! It's getting late.
CLEMENTE: My truthful tongue will bit by bit dispel
      all doubt concerning why I supplicate.
CRESPO: Speak: I was never deaf nor am I now.

CLEMENTE: From my earliest years,
      guided by the star that rules my fate,
      and unclouded by deceit,
      I've gazed with adoration upon the sun
      that this veil conceals:
      this is what whoever gazes on her feels.

      Her rays impressed themselves
      upon the best part of my heart that they
      transformed my heart to rays:
      I'm all afire and fire is all I am
      and yet withal I freeze
      since by my sun's eclipse a veil is all I see.

      Free reciprocation
      did my unblemished pure desire receive,
      for love permitted me
      to put my heart to use with rich effect;
      and so you may infer
      this shepherdess loves me, as I love her.

Without her father knowing –
he plays the tyrant with her liberty
because she has no mother –
she pledged her hand and swore to be my wife;
now fear and dread combine
to make her scared to tell him that she's mine.

[He's rich and so she's scared
he'll be offended by my humble means:
for in this tyr'nnous age,
the habit makes the monk not the reverse;
though he's richer than me,
by nature I'm as well-endowed as he.]

I might not be as rich,
but I'm just as good and match his wealth
by always keeping clear
of all depravity and idle vice:
and in good people's eyes,
virtue, not money, is the greater prize.

I ask that she agree
again to be my wife in front of you,
resolving so to be
without fearing what her papa might do,
for those who are joined under
God's good grace, let no man put asunder.

CRESPO: What does the sun reply
      that hides in clouds in this unseasonable way?
CLEMENTE: She will not testify,
      unless by signals I regret to say –
      her conduct is so modest –
      and thus she'll make her meaning manifest.

CRESPO: Girl, did you plight your troth?
CLEMENTE: She bows her head which means in semaphore
      she won't deny the oath.
SANCHO: So, Señor Judge, what are we waiting for?

CRESPO: For Pedro to withdraw
    a sentence from my hood that is all.

    And then we'll hear it read.
PEDRO: This sentence will be right – no ifs and buts –
    And I have always said:
    though it may come by detours or short cuts
    the truth will be believed.
    So will this sentence be, which I now read:

PEDRO takes a paper from the hood and reads it out.

    'I Martín Crespo hereby declare,
    The stallion shall always get his mare.'

REDONDO: It's like a lucky dip, that hood of yours –
    a marvel of a judgement just came out –
    and though it deals with what goes on all fours
    it almost seems that it's been thought about.
CLEMENTE: My knee falls to the earth, my soul soars
    to God, I kiss your knee as a devout
    who sees it as a column that supports
    the edifice that's home to all wise thoughts.

CRESPO: Even if the sentence went so far
    as giving you my very soul, my boy –
    I mean by that my daughter Clemency –
    it still would bring me pleasure and great joy.
    (*To CLEMENCIA.*) So let us now enjoy your presence here,
    which is only courteous and right;
    since the judgement I've just melted out
    will be implemented without a doubt.

CLEMENCIA: Then with that assurance, oh my father,
    I now take off the veil and at your feet
    prostrate myself – why do you turn away?
    I am your daughter not some dreadful monster.
    You gave the sentence of your own free will!
    If it's unjust then you must take the blame;

but if it's just then see that it's approved,
that all impediments may be removed.

CRESPO: What I wrote is written, well said daughter.
This boy shall be my lawful wedded son;
from this trial the whole world ought 'a
know law not passion ruled what I've done.

SANCHO: Every person here is your supporter
In the unexpected joy that you have won.

TARUGO: And every tongue is praising Crespo too,
that clever man who knows just what to do.

PEDRO: Master you should understand
what a special grace it is,
one that heaven can grant a man,
whenever it disposes
to give him a good woman's hand.

She too will gain from the pairing,
if the man with whom she's sharing
her bed is someone virile,
good natured, with a ready smile,
not hot headed – more forbearing.

Clemente and Clemency
are going to make a happy pair;
they'll bring you much felicity
and ensure that there are heirs
with your noble pedigree.

And on this night of St John –
a good night to celebrate on –
how their wedding will make you gay!

CRESPO: You show by everything you say,
that you never put a foot wrong.

[But since this night is occupied
with celebrating generally,
let their marriage be sanctified
another day.

CLEMENTE: That's fine with me,
in thought she's already my bride.

It seems to me the heart's delight
consists in hope for what's in sight
and not just in possession.

PEDRO: Diligence and shrewd discretion
there's nothing that they can't put right.]

CRESPO: Let's go we still have much to do,
the night is young!

TARUGO: Well said, well said!

CLEMENTE: Now you're my wife and mistress too
there's nothing left for me to dread,
my hopes and dreams have all come true.

TARUGO: How well you've chosen, Clemency!

CLEMENCIA: He who arranged all this, it's he
that I must thank and God as well.

PEDRO: It was no angel, truth to tell
who performed this agency.

All exit apart from PEDRO.
Enter MALDONADO, the gypsy chief. *

MALDONADO: May God keep you Pedro, Señor,
It's you that I've come looking for:
Tell me now, how you are faring?
I want to see if you're daring
or still a coward as before?

Do you want to go ahead
and join our band as a comrade,
to be our companion and friend?

---

*   In the Spanish text this scene comes after the scene between Pedro and Pascual
following Roque's four line soliloquy – it was moved to allow the Pascual/
Benita story to be uninterrupted.

PEDRO: Yes I do.

MALDONADO: Does it depend............?

    You have a doubt?

PEDRO: No, not a shred!

MALDONADO: Look Pedro, the life we lead
       is free and easy, unrestrained,
       enquiring, leisurely and long,
       a life in which you can attain
       every desire, every penchant.

    The grassy earth provides a bed,
    the sky that arches overhead
    provides us with a pavilion.
    We're not scorched by the blazing sun;
    the freezing cold we do not dread.

    No orchard wall is built so high
    that when the fruits begin to swell
    we can't get in and take supplies.
    The albilla grape or Moscatel
    as soon as they materialise –

    quick as a flash they're contraband
    in the daring gypsy's hand;
    he's a lynx with other's fruit,
    he's wily, spirited and acute,
    loose-limbed, agile, healthy to boot.

    And when the fruits of love appear
    our enjoyment is the same,
    for there are no rivals here,
    and so we're warmed by love's hot flame
    without jealousy or fear.

    In our camp is to be found
    a girl determined to turn down
    every suitor; she's so fair,

that even the envious declare
that her perfection is profound.

A gypsy woman who stole her
brought her to us. If you'd seen her
you'd be certain of her worth
from her beauty and demeanour;
no lovelier girl trod this earth.

This girl shall belong to you
Pedro. What ever she may do
to flee the yoke, she will yield
as soon as the accord is sealed
of the friendship between us two.

PEDRO: Maldonado, that you may see
    why it is my firm intention
    to change my whole identity,
    will you give me your attention
    for a moment?
MALDONADO: Certainly.

PEDRO: This story you're about to hear
    is going to make it very clear
    if I'm cut out for gypsy ways.
MALDONADO: Begin your tale! No more delays!
    And I'll lend an attentive ear.

PEDRO: Left on a doorstep as they say
    I never knew my father's name,
    where I came from, a sad, sad fate!
    A heavy weight on my life!
    Who took me in, I haven't a clue,
    but what I do know is this boy got
    indoctrinated by the brothers;
    I was like all those others, those scabby
    shabby boys, learning to pray
    and to starve all day because
    they don't give you food there

but they do give lashings away.
At the same time, I'm learning
how to read and write and I'm
learning how to lie and be fly like a fox,
learning how to steal from the collection box.
But as I got bigger this life
got too small. So I followed the call
of the sea; I decided to be
a cabin boy going to the Indies
and back, in a ship, in a fleet,
in my rough linen shirt and
trousers the same covered in tar,
with not a penny to my name.
I was frightened in the doldrums,
and when a storm was at its height.
With Bermuda in sight
I was terrified.
Lost the taste for charred dry bread,
put an end to drinking rations;
that devilish wine'll bring final reunion
with your Maker and last communion!
So once again I am near the banks
of the river Guadalquivir
and thanks to its swelling flow
back to Seville I go,
where I fill the role –
it's a base vile one but still –
of a thieving delivery boy –
no choice but to enter that employ!
and though I'm not a priest, at least
I was able to collect many tithes
and besides save many things from going astray,
for which I may be judged some day.
But then this job was suspended,
a slight mishap ended it and I had
to become the lad of a bad man,
a ruffian; dangerous work!

It taught me about the rough life
out there in the underworld, how to stir up strife,
spreading rumours in the wind,
making a whisper deadlier than a knife.
My master was a master
of the art of picking pockets;
his attack on them was violent,
it was deadly, it was silent.
But he was caught red handed
by an arm of the law –
on the rack he turned confessor,
saw the light like St Paul, but lacked
the martyr's call, I mean calling.

MALDONADO: Call it 'call' or 'calling' and
call him Saul or Paul, just don't start
spouting Latin or Greek that's all.

PEDRO: For his sins he got a flogging
much to the chagrin of the hangdog
hangman, who's still downcast!
I was told so by a grass.
Alas my master was taken
to the galleys and many Sally's
in the alleys, many women of the street,
wept and in despair tore their hair.
So no longer under the care
of my knight from Andalucia,
I was forced to be a bearer
for a soldier on manoeuvres,
who was a rascal of the kind
who was minded to stay behind
when called on to advance unless
he was being advanced his pay.
I caught chickens that deserted!
And from vouchers for our lodgings I made profits untold!
Woe is me, if heaven won't pardon
these deeds when they're told.
That life taught me a lesson –

what a slap in the face it gave –
I learnt the malingering soldier
also ends up a galley slave.
So I took a post on the coast
as an exciseman where I was heir
to a thousand piratical shocks
but with ten thousand perks to spare.
But to allay my fears that I
might be abducted to Algiers,
I fled to Cordoba and made
my living selling orangeade
and firewater, but drank away
my month's wages in a day:
for the fire burns your money
'cos you spend it like water.
My master threw me out,
waved a gun in my face.
I ended up, by misfortune,
in an Asturian's place.
He made waffles for selling,
so it was waffles I sold,
but I wagered my waffles
and lost ten basketfuls.
When I left, I met a blind man,
and I served him ten months too,
if only those months had been years,
I'd know more than Merlin ever knew.
I learnt to speak the patter,
how to be a blind man's eyes,
how with genteel graceful language
to make prayers that solemnise.
But then my good old blind man
died and left me, like Saint Paul,
penniless but wiser,
clear-sighted and sharp withal.
So then I was a mule-boy
and then a cardsharp's lad –

this cad confused you by losing
then pounced when you followed suit.
He'd conjure tricks out of nowhere:
with a single hand I've seen him deal
blows on his foes that made them reel
and feel stumped by the thumps of his trumps.
Bumps and indentations, smudges
and notches and crenellations
were tricks that were all on the cards,
and polishing them till they dazzled,
and other devilish high jinks.
Even a lynx wearing the specs of El Cid
would be hoodwinked and not perceive
what he concealed up his sleeve.
The whole pack collapsed one day
and he had to throw in his hand:
they labelled him a cheat and hung
a card around him like a brand.
So I left him and came here
to the countryside, as you see,
to serve Martín Crespo, the mayor,
who loves himself less than he loves me.
I call myself Pedro the Great
but a fortune-teller read my hand,
foretold my fate from the lines
he saw in the palm and stated,
'Pedro add to that word 'Great',
the word 'Pretender'; you will be
a king, a pope, a friar as well,
the figure that leads the carnival.
And through a gypsy, I foretell,
there's something that will befall you,
that King and Queen will take great joy
in hearing and in listening to.
Though you'll have many heavy jobs
for you there's only one career,
which, at the end, will let you be

everything I've told you here.'
And although I don't believe him,
still I sense deep down inside,
an inclination to become
all that I heard prophesied.
His prediction may be fiction,
but it's manifest in you,
I declare, from this time forth,
I'm going to be a gypsy too.

MALDONADO: Magnanimous Pedro and Great Pretender,
the heart and column of the gypsy temple!
Come, initiate this noble plan,
which prompts and moves you, drives you, bears you on
to place yourself on the gypsy roll.
Come and soften the hard but tender heart
of her I've spoken of, that stolen girl,
who'll render you the happiest of men!
PEDRO: I have no doubt the outcome will be so,
I have the highest hopes of it, let's go.

*As they go PASCUAL enters and tugs PEDRO's smock – the two
of them remain onstage. After a while, ROQUE, a sexton, enters.*

PASCUAL: Pedro, my friend.
PEDRO: What's up, Pascual?
I've not forgotten what I said.
I'll sort things out for you. I shall!
I've nothing else in my head
but how I'm going to help my pal.

Now look, tonight is St John's Eve
and all the girls round here believe
that on this night they'll know their fate,
and who is going to be their mate,
by special signs that they'll receive.

Benita with uncovered head
and her feet placed in a basin

full of water, listening hard,
until dawn will be awaiting
a sign to tell her whom she'll wed.

In her street you must say
your name, Pascual, in such a way
that she can clearly hear the sound.
PASCUAL: How well you deserve your renown!
What ingenuity you display!

[Fear not, I'll be advised by you,
but afterwards, I think there might
be something else for you to do,
for Cupid's fire could catch alight
and start to burn in your chest too.]

PEDRO: Alright – farewell in God's good name.
PASCUAL goes.
ROQUE: You think you're fly, but all the same,
I'll get there ahead of you
then I'll see what I can do
to beat you both at your own game.

Exit ROQUE.
BENITA appears at the window with her hair loose (as a virgin).

BENITA: Oh night, spread your wings over all
who speak of love to you, hear their calls,
attend to their just demands,
for it's said that even the Moors
celebrate you in foreign lands.

I let my hair blow in the wind
to achieve what I intend,
in this basin where I have put
clear cool water, I place my foot,
and listen for signs the air may send.

It's said, wherever she's confined,
the girl who listens all night through

will receive a lucky sign
from the voice that sounds within you,
oh night so sacred and divine.

May my ears, which are so keen,
hear a name from which I'll glean
that my future's looking good.*
ROQUE: Roque's the name, rook if you would,
tonight the castle takes the Queen!

Rook will be the man to take
the lovely lady in this game;
whatever move she might make,
his fate says that it's he who'll claim
the richest prize and no mistake.

BENITA: Rook is spoken and Rook I hear,
but the only rook round here
is that idiot the sexton;
let's see what is said next an'
if it's Rook again.
ROQUE: It's Rook, my dear,

No lady escapes Rook's designs,
no knight can effect her release,
she yields her beauty and resigns,
and he's a valuable piece
though he moves within narrow lines.

BENITA: Psst, take this ribbon, good Sir,
it's the one that you must wear
tomorrow so I will know you.
ROQUE: I will do it, and faithfully too,
Oh most lovely and most fair!

*As BENITA is giving the ribbon to ROQUE, PASCUAL enters,
grips him round the neck and takes the ribbon from him.*

---

*   Benita's whole speech is sung in the RSC version.

There are two ladies living there
and whichever one you might be
I know that Venus can't compare
with you.

PASCUAL: My eyes must be deceived!
Such conduct! How do you dare?

Benita, I just can't believe
you'd let this Sexton receive
your favour. It's a grave abuse!
You'd not have the least excuse
if tonight weren't Saint John's Eve.

And you, a bachelor in the art
of singing plainsong, what professor
instructed you in this part,
so you'd know enough of the score,
to outplay us, you upstart?

Can the matin bell be rung
by such a brazen shameless one?
You've forgotten how to sing
and how to make the church bells ring,
because of what this mad girl's done?

PEDRO enters.

PEDRO: Pascual, is something untoward?
PASCUAL: The sexton and Benita request
that I'm a witness to record,
that like her name she is bless'd
and he's an enemy to fraud.

To show him that he's in the soup,
and prove how low he will stoop
in carrying out his intent,
as evidence I here present
this ribbon and this nincompoop.

ROQUE: It's the holy cruet I now swear by,
      which every day with great attention
      I wipe spotless and leave bone-dry,
      that it was never my intention
      to mock the truth or tell a lie!

      Today I heard the two of you
      say what Benita planned to do
      up there, with her hair let down,
      so, señores, I came around,
      to enjoy the fiesta too.

      I said my name and like a bird
      she quickly answered my decoy,
      as if the man whose name she heard
      personified well being and joy,
      all her future in that first word.

      That superstitious sorcery
      used by girls customarily
      on the night before St John's Act
      only goes to show that they
      are creatures of vain fantasy.

PASCUAL: So why did you take her ribbon?
ROQUE: So that I could put it on;
      so that its appearance might
      let her know I was the one
      in the morning when it grew light!

BENITA: Why don't you tell me why you ask
      all these questions, Pascual? Why cast
      aspersions? But then I've always found,
      though never slow to run me down,
      you're quick in taking me to task.

PASCUAL: Ungrateful girl, can this be true?
      For this your heart should be torn out!
      You question my love for you?

Its sincerity's not in doubt,
it's unique, to give it its due.

Down by the river you can see
your name carved in the poplar trees
by my knife; ask them, they'll say
if I'm a man whose behaviour may
be lacking in propriety.

PEDRO: And in that meadow it's the same,
where every beech tree is inscribed
and crowned, Benita, with your name.
I've seen it with my own two eyes!
They all seek to enhance your fame.

PASCUAL: Where shepherds gather I'd aspire –
I'm sure you never saw me tire –
to praise Benita to the sky,
showing my devotion thereby,
without baseness in my desire.

What almond, apple or cherry tree
have you seen bearing early fruit
that my hand did not pick and carry
to your fair hand as a tribute
so that the birds flew fruitlessly.

The branches that will come to dress
your bowered doorway presently –
you must admit, cruel murderess,
how clearly in them you will see
the faith that's dwelling in my breast.

You're sure to see verbena there,
bringing friendship beyond compare;
and the rose, to bring happiness;
and – this bodes well for success –
the palm with its triumphant air.

You'll see those slender fronds that hang
from the stately poplar tree
brought from the valley so they might
shade your door from the burning sun
and give your senses sheer delight.

BENITA: Your harangue will not convince me
to touch your hand amorously –
of that there should be no mistake
tor the only spouse I can take
will be a man called Rook or Roque.

PEDRO: You're right to be so obstinate,
the remedy is very plain –
no more need to equivocate –
for the holy Confirmation
gives us the answer on a plate!

Pascual can get himself confirmed
and change his name so that instead
of Pascual he'll be Rook and so
to his delight and your relief,
the two of you can then be wed.

BENITA: If it's done so, then I say, 'Yes'.
ROQUE: Thanks be to God with all my heart
that I've escaped from such a mess.
PEDRO: I vow you're being very smart
Benita, when you acquiesce.

[There's a proverb that says it all
by which good people set a store,
because it shows a lot of nous,
'If you want a man about the house,
just go and grab the boy next door.']

BENITA: Pascual, you must wear this ribbon,
make sure it's somewhere I can see.
PASCUAL: I'll make it a precious possession

as Iris turns her livery
into a treasure in the heaven.

Wait! The music's starting to sound
that accompanies the parade,
when the branches are brought around.

PEDRO: We'll gladly stay to hear it played!

BENITA: I welcome it so let it sound!

*All kinds of music within including Zamoran bagpipes. Enter as
many as possible carrying branches – principally CLEMENTE;
enter, too, MUSICIANS singing the following:* *

MUSICIANS: *Girl on the balcony,*
   or there behind bars,
   the love you are waiting for,
   stands just outside your door.

   Oh night of St John,
   he who came before,
   whose hands told the time
   better than a clock's,
   his saintly finger told
   that the day was here,
   when light came to the world
   and night would fall no more;
   reveal yourself to us,
   and may the dawn pour
   dewdrops that shine like pearls
   upon every flower
   and while you are waiting
   for the rising sun,
   tell my girl in tones
   that no discord mars:

   Girl on the balcony,
   or there behind bars,

---

* See Appendix for lyrics used in the RSC production.

the love you are waiting for,
stands just outside your door.

Tell Benita 'tis she
that Pascual adores
he's shepherd to the love
that pastures in his heart.
Tell Clemency as well
that he who's her lord
is her most humble slave,
it's written in the stars;
and don't forget the girl
who starts to lose heart
in what she wishes for,
take her hand in yours
and whisper to her low,
or raise your voice high
so that in her yearnings
she must hear your calls:

Girl on the balcony,
or there behind bars,
the love you are waiting for,
stands just outside your door.

CLEMENTE: The singing of the song was good.
Come let's put around this portal
some of the branches we've supplied –
what are you doing here Pascual,
with these two others at your side?

Help us here to woo Benita,
we'll both serve and entreat her
by putting branches round her door:
even if affection's dying
that will be revivifying.

Let's put the laurel on this side
and the willow on the other

and place the white poplar here,
and between them let the jasmine
and the gillyflower appear.

Sedge will turn the ground to em'rald
and then the petals of the woad
will render it a rich topaz
In between let's festoon garlands
so that every space is filled.

BENITA: Please let the music play again, Señores,
so Clemency may hear it too and you (*To PASCUAL.*)
my Rook,

She leaves the window.

must make it sound again.

PASCUAL: Alright,
sweet instrument of my confirmation.
The jingling tambourines shall sound once more,
the guitars shall be strummed and flourishes
be played again; let's solemnise this morn,
that's celebrated throughout the world,
for it's the wish of her, whom I revere.

CLEMENTE: Sing on, and then let's go, the day is near!

MUSICIANS: *The thorns and brambles placed*
in my sweet love's bower,
each one of them shall be
turned into a flower.
The ash with his rough bark
and the mighty oak,
when placed at the door
of her who is my life,
will see themselves become
sacred scented groves,
transformed by her glance
so great is its power.
Each one of them shall be
turned into a flower.

Where'er she rests her eyes,
or puts her gentle foot,
there the grass grows green,
which was withered before.
For her, the fields are gay,
she gladdens every heart,
serfs fall for her charms,
and their lordships cower.
Each one of them shall be
turned into a flower.

They exit singing.
Enter INÉS and BELICA, gypsy girls.

INÉS: It's all fantasy, Belilla
I really don't know what to say:
you either dream you're a countess
or else you're mistress to the king!
BELICA: It might just be dreams, that's the thing!

Inés; don't incur my anger
with your scolding and rebukes;
Why not let me follow my star?
INÉS: So confident in your beauty
you think you're better than you are!

Beauty without eminence will
never bring a girl good fortune.
Why can't you get that in your head?
BELICA: My eminent misfortune
confirms everything you've said.

Why was fate so harsh and cruel
to give a gypsy girl who's poor
such a rich imagination?
INÉS: You're building castles in the air
and that air's beyond your station.

Have done with these fantasies;
come and finish learning the dance
that you started recently.

BELICA: Inés, you are destroying me
with this argumentative stance.

But you're mistaken if you think
I'm to be ruled by your volition
and take your every word as law,
there's only one I'll do it for,
and that's the King, I'll dance for him.

INÉS: Belilla I won't be surprised
if you're institutionalised
for carrying on in this way;
the leading lady's not a part
that girls like you are meant to play.

What's wrong with dancing in the parlour
or the kitchen for heaven's sake;
or wherever else you might be?

BELICA: I'm sorry that's just not for me.

INÉS: What then? Fine clothes, airs and graces,

pomp and circumstance, coats of arms?
You'd tear down the gypsy banner
that through our honest graft we raised
to the heavens? And you'd desert?
You'd drag our standard through the dirt?

I would rather see you driven,
mad or else see you given
to a gypsy who would break you,
see the executioner take you,
and measure you for your coffin.

This wicked gypsy girl believes
she's too good for a gypsy lad!

It's enough to make you rave!
Girl, if you're going to be so bad,
go dig yourself an early grave.

BELICA: You ramble so long-windedly;
you're a fool, you can't foretell,
where my plans are leading me.

INÉS: I see the future very well,
however foolish I might be

Enter PEDRO and MALDONADO.

MALDONADO: Pedro my friend, that gypsy girl,
whose sublime looks I have mentioned,
remember her? Well there she stands!
She's the one it's my intention
to deliver into your hands.

Change your clothes immediately
and learn our language fluently
though I think you very fit
to be a gypsy without it.
You'll soon head a new dynasty.

INÉS: Most handsome gentleman may I
ask if you have alms to spare?

MALDONADO: A working man's not impressed by
that sort of talk, you've blundered there
Inés!

INÉS: So let Belica try.

PEDRO: No matter what request this maid
might make, I swear she'll be obeyed,
nothing's too much trouble for me;
if I'm allowed to serve this beauty
I'll think that I am amply paid.

MALDONADO: Señora, won't you answer him?

INÉS: My Gypsy Chief, that widow's there,

the tight-fisted one who's so grim,
in getting more and hoarding more,
although her cup's full to the brim.

MARINA (a widowed farmer) enters led by the hand by
LLORENTE, her SQUIRE (also of farming stock).

INÉS: My Lady, have you alms for me
in the name of bléssed Mary,
and in her son's name also bless'd?

MARINA: I'm never moved by the request
for alms, or by importunity.

Surely it is preferable
for you girls to enter service
than to beg which I think shameful.

LLORENTE: The state of the world's so parlous
it's simply intolerable.

It's a time of tramps and vagrants:
no girl wants to be a servant,
no boy works to earn his bread,
he treads the primrose path instead.
He's a fool and she's arrogant.

This sponging crowd's always looking
to perpetrate misdeeds and crime,
double dealing, shifty, cunning,
they pay no tithes at harvest time,
and pay no homage to the king.

The felonies that they commit
aren't detected – that world's unlit;
I hope the word won't cause offence,
but no tether on your ass prevents
the gypsy thief from rustling it.

MARINA: It's getting late so leave them be,
Squire, let's be on our way!

51

LLORENTE and MARINA exit.

BELICA: You can keep your charity!
　　By doing that, you just display
　　your neediness and poverty

　　to the likes of them; you'll find too
　　there will always be a Squire
　　to persecute and slander you
　　and no matter if your needs are dire,
　　he won't give you a single sou.

MALDONADO: You see her Pedro? It is said,
　　she keeps two bolted chests beside
　　her at the bottom of her bed,
　　with ten thousand ducats inside,
　　but which she calls angels instead.

　　She kneels and worships them in prayer
　　as if she puts her glory there;
　　when she sees them she's in raptures,
　　it's as if her feeling captures
　　Absalom's feeling for his hair.

　　Just once a month she gives away
　　to a blind man one sovereign.
　　He comes every morning to pray
　　at her door, thus offering
　　to the heavenly court each day

　　pleas for grace and expiation,
　　so her husband and relations,
　　languishing in purgatory,
　　will be deemed worthy of glory
　　in that holy adjudication.

　　With just this one good work she thinks
　　she's going to go straight up to heaven
　　without ado and without sin.

PEDRO: Let me shake her up a bit
      with my cleverness and wit.

      Maldonado, you must discover
      every name of every brother,
      sister, uncle, aunt and dear one,
      every friend and every near one,
      every last servant or other;

      write them down and bring them to me,
      I'll free her from her stinginess
      I shall do it easily;
      I shall make this hoax the test
      of my ingenuity.

MALDONADO: I'll bring you the most exact list
      of all her kin who are deceased,
      from the smallest little laddy
      down to her great great granddaddy,
      not a hair there will be missed.

PEDRO: You're going to be very impressed
      by the way that I will cheat her
      in everybody's interest.
MALDONADO: Where are you going now Belica?
BELICA: I'm leaving that up to Inés.

PEDRO: Your lofty thoughts will be your guide
      and I'm sure that they'll provide
      a fitting end that's noble, where –
BELICA: Maybe they're castles in the air
      these desires! But don't deride

      and mock them Pedro, 'good my Sire',
      for I see shining from afar
      a hope that's burning like a fire –
      maybe it's my guiding star –
      bringing me that to which I aspire.

PEDRO: Such beauty deserves reward
   and the fortune it will afford
   should equal it. Rare gypsy maid,
   the age gives you its accolade;
   in you its glory is assured!

Exeunt.

End of the First Act.

ACT TWO

*Enter a MASTER OF THE REVELS and MARTÍN CRESPO,
the mayor and SANCHO MACHO, the alderman.**

CRESPO: Master of the Revels, he quit,
      this Pedro lad of whom I talk,
      he could invent, I'm sure of it,
      a marvel from a cabbage stalk –
      so sharp and clever is his wit.

      He told me if by any chance
      the king should ask to see some dance,
      the one that I present must be
      so pretty that it exceeds
      all others in its radiance.

      'Dancing maidens! Don't employ them!'
      is what he then went on to say,
      'For the King just won't enjoy them –
      to him they're terribly passé –
      all dancing masters deploy them!'

      Rather I should climb new peaks
      by using lads who should compete
      dressed as lasses from the hills
      with lots of little tinkling bells
      tied around their arms and feet.

      Already I've two dozen of them
      all kitted out that way;
      I wouldn't be ashamed to see 'em
      transported and put on display
      in the Roman Coliseum.

*   and in the RSC production DIEGO TARUGO, DIEGO -FLY-THE-COOP
     and GIL THE CARDER.

DIEGO AND GIL perform a dance.

> These are two of the very best
> of my troupe.*

MASTER: I have to confess
> that it's quite an innovation.

SANCHO: Around here our mayor's creations
> are known for their unusualness.

> His ingenuity he owes
> to that clever serving lad,
> who taught him everything he knows,
> but then left us. It's too bad –
> a plague on him for doing so!

> Without him we find we lose
> our cleverness and spirit too.

MASTER: He's so clever?

SANCHO: And so wise!
> He would even be lionised
> by Solomon King of the Jews.

CRESPO: You've just seen a little fraction
> of the lads. There are twenty four.
> I guarantee satisfaction
> from the rest – they're straight and tall,
> hale, hearty, ready for action.

> That one neither limps nor stoops,
> his name is Diego-Fly-the-Coop;
> the other's called Gil the Carder,
> both perform with skill and ardour,
> they dance like dogs who jump through hoops.

---

*   The Spanish text has no dance at this point and the speech reads:
> You've seen two of the very best
> already.

Pingalong is accompanist,
but they'll show their agility
no matter what the rhythm is
and they'll prove indisputably
how great our innovation is.

There'll be no sword dances today,
just this maidenly display,
but they'll do it so skilfully
we'll make the gypsies green with envy
and put real girls in disarray.

Weren't you impressed by the figures
of the two that you've just seen?
Both of them can dance with vigour.

MASTER: The impression they made has been
    so terrible, it made me snigger.

If you take that path, sad to say,
on your return you'll lose your way,
you'll be in such a sorry state.

CRESPO: Señor, that serves to illustrate
    that your jealousy holds sway.

I'm going to take, I say again,
twenty-four lads dressed as maidens
just like those two, for I maintain
that such clever innovations
inspire wonder and entertain.

MASTER: God be with you if you do.
   He goes.

SANCHO: Señor Mayor, you must be true
    to your taste and the proof will be
    that the king will find diversion
    in this dance because it's new.

CRESPO: Doubtless! Let's go in any case!
    It makes my heart quicken its pace,

> thinking how the dance will earn
> applause there, Sancho.

SANCHO: You'll return
> with a smile upon your face.

Exeunt.

Enter two BLIND MEN, one of which is PEDRO. The first one approaches a door and PEDRO stands beside him. The widow MARINA comes to the window.

BLIND MAN: Oh you souls that fortune looks on,
> now languishing in purgat'ry,
> receive from God your consolation
> and know that very soon you'll leave
> that place of pain and damnation;
> thunder will resound,
> and the good angel will come down
> raising you for coronation.

PEDRO: Oh you souls of this house from where
> some departed on a stool
> and others in a plush armchair,
> may the divine tribunal rule
> that you're spotless beyond compare,
> and in one fell swoop
> may the good angel raise you up,
> so you'll see what's going on up there.

BLIND MAN: Brother, go pray at another door;
> this house is mine and I regret
> your prayers will get you nothing here.

PEDRO: I don't pray for what I can get,
> it's out of courtesy I call
> and therefore I may
> pray wherever I want to pray
> without a dispute or a brawl.

BLIND MAN: You've a whole sight of tricks maybe,
    honoured Blind Man?
PEDRO: I've been entombed
    since birth in dark obscurity.
BLIND MAN: Once I had sight but I was doomed
    to lose it, God has punished me.
    Now I can't see a thing,
    unless it's something displeasing
    which is what the accursèd see.

    You know a lot of prayers, do you?
PEDRO: [So many prayers I can recall,
    this is no boast, I swear it's true:
    I give out copies to one and all,
    and those I hide them from are few;]

    I know one for the spirit and there's
    St Pancras's prayer, efficacious
    in warding off rape; I know prayers
    of Saints Quirce and Acacious,
    and Spanish Eulalia, where
    the verse is sublime,
    and the expression so divine,
    they've refinement beyond compare.

    [Prayers for the dying? No problem!
    There're thirty of them I can say.
    And others I know are such gems,
    that all other people who pray
    are angry and jealous of them;
    wherever I am,
    it's goes like this ad nauseam,
    because I'm la crème de la crème.]

    I know one for boils and lesions,
    one that will cure you of jaundice,
    one for scrofulous eruptions
    and one that tempers avarice

in the heart of the greediest person;
and in fact, I know
a prayer to heal any woe
brought on by internal passion,

or else by inquisitiveness.
I know so many, I'm in thrall
to their virtue and goodness.

BLIND MAN. How I'm longing to hear them all!

MARINA: Brother, wait there, I'm impressed!

PEDRO: Who is calling me?

BLIND MAN: From the voice it must be she,
the mistress here at this address.

Although she's rich, she's tight-fisted,
and her charity's confined
to paying for prayers to be said.

PEDRO: If she's not generously inclined
I'm not inclined to talk, instead
I'll stay quite dumb.
If she begs me I'll keep mum
like a stone that won't be bled.

MARINA enters.

MARINA: From up there at my casement
I heard how you professed your faith,
how you reasoned, all your statements,
and the many prayers you say
will cure all ills and ailments.

Do me the favour I request
of loaning me some of the best
prayers you have in your possession,
leaving it to my discretion
how much money I'll invest.

PEDRO: (*Secretly to her/aside.*) If you're discreet, dismiss this other,
then you'll hear marv'llous things from me.

MARINA: *(Secretly to him/aside.)* I'll dismiss him, my good brother.
PEDRO: *(Aloud.)* Señora not for love or money
  can I tell them to another.

MARINA: Go now and return by and by,
  good friend.
BLIND MAN: As usual I
will come to pray on the stroke of three.
MARINA: Alright.
BLIND MAN: Your blindness may be
a blind or maybe not, goodbye.

  But if we are to stay in touch
  come to my house and there you'll see,
  though it's shabby, poor, without much
  room that most indubitably,
  in goodwill, it's extremely rich.

  There'll be a bonus there also,
  which will gladden your heart I know;
  I'll give you a mountain of tips,
  if you just open your lips
  and let your wonderful prayers flow.

PEDRO: I will come by, very well,
  and visit your honoured abode
  where so much love and good faith dwell
  and I'll pay you any rent that's owed
  with what I teach and what I tell.

  [Forty miracles I bring
  with me, in my toing and froing,
  wherever I happen to be,
  I pass my time most happily
  and live my life just like a king.]

The BLIND MAN exits.

  Señora Marina of the clan
  of Sánchez, let your ear incline,

listen to my voice, so you can
hear this embassy divine,
that's brought to you by mortal man.

When souls in purgatory went
to undergo final judgement,
they wisely specified
that their kin should be notified
of their unbearable torment

And this was to be accomplished,
by arranging that one of them,
who was prudent and judicious,
should take the form of an old man
and return to the world like this,

he should instruct these relations
and give a lengthy narration,
explaining what they have to do,
so these lost souls might accrue
if not pardon, then alleviation.

[This soul is near here already,
with a body that is old and honest,
as far as I myself can see.
He's bringing with him on an ass,
the mined treasures of Potosí.]

For on hearing that there exist
souls in Purgat'ry on this list,
grieving at the pains they suffer,
there's not a purse, desk or coffer
that is able to resist.

So he comes laden with doubloons,
which those relatives have donated
in piles for their kindred's souls,
whose torment is unabated,
in the Passions they undergo.

[Even the most guarded purse
pregnant with its coins of gold
can be induced and is most willing,
to give birth down here to what it holds
and free souls up there from suffering.]

Señora Marina this soul
is coming here this afternoon
so that he can let you know
who on the list is close to you.
But you should keep it secret though.

He asks that he be received
alone and everything the bereaved
request, you be prepared to give,
else in those fires where they live
they've no hope of being relieved.

He promises when this is done
he'll teach you one of his prayers
to bring you money by the ton.
He'll do this, he declares,
to reward the goodwill of one

who showed him so candidly
she'd rip her very last ha'penny
from its hiding place and remain
without a penny to her name,
like Paul, who was both poor and saintly.

MARINA: This is the task from the divine
that this soul brings me to complete?
PEDRO: All the details you will find
written out in the receipt
which your relatives have signed.

MARINA: How will this soul be recognised
when it arrives?

PEDRO: I'll contrive
        that he looks a lot like me.
MARINA: You'll be rewarded handsomely
        for you deserve such a prize!

PEDRO: [In things like this it's best to spend
        money that's been saved before;
        all that scrupulous fasting,
        getting whipped till your back was raw,
        are just means to this useful end.]

        Nothing ventured nothing gained.
        You must give all till naught remains
        to take a soul from agony
        and bring it to a territ'ry,
        where there's no suffering or pain.

MARINA: Go in peace; tell this old man
        that I await him happily;
        when he's here I'll put in his hand
        all my soul, I mean my money,
        with humble heart of a Christian.

        And though I am a little thrifty
        with money, I would hate to see
        even one of my relations
        undergoing the depredations
        of fire and cold eternally.

PEDRO: May your fame exceed Leander's
        may your generous heart remain
        as unrivalled as Alexander's,
        may it be praised in a swan's refrain
        on the waters of Maeander,

        may it pass to hyperborean
        mountains. You too are heaven-bound,
        so that with it you ascend and
        in the circle of our horizon
        another like it won't be found.

The two of them exit.
Enter MALDONADO and BELICA.

MALDONADO: Look, Belica, that's the man
　　　　who'll help you up a rung or two,
　　　　he has wit and reputation,
　　　　when you see what he's prepared to do,
　　　　he's bound to earn your admiration.

　　　　To win your love he's agreed
　　　　to become a gypsy and he'd
　　　　give up everything for you.
　　　　It's only right, you must concede,
　　　　that *you* be openhearted too.

　　　　He'll be the best of cattle-thieves
　　　　that the world has ever seen –
　　　　that is as far as I can tell –
　　　　the most unmatched, original,
　　　　and rare trickster there's ever been.

　　　　There's a trick he's got in mind
　　　　that shows clearly in its design
　　　　he'll be unique amongst con men!
BELICA: How quickly you arrange things when
　　　　it's to your taste and not to mine.

　　　　Is it not clear? Are you so dense?
　　　　I've said the man is not for me
　　　　who can't raise me to eminence.
MALDONADO: Nothing proves more conclusively
　　　　that you're lacking commonsense

　　　　than this fantasy of yours,
　　　　which youthful graces reinforce
　　　　now that you have them in profusion –
　　　　but that fade sooner than the sun
　　　　which takes one day to run its course.

[Obviously it's craziness,
pure and simple, that you display,
if you think your loveliness
can last longer than the day,
which the night obscures in darkness.

And what's more it's pure stupidity
to think that physical beauty
is going to deliver a match,
who will be deemed a better catch,
than one brought by equality.]

Mad gypsy girl stop these daydreams
and rein in your grand desire
that both exalts you and demeans
and don't go looking to acquire
something that's beyond your means.

Take an equal when you marry.
Such a husband he'll prove to be –
this man that I now offer you –
and with him I'm offering too
wealth, honour and integrity.

Enter PEDRO who has now changed into gypsy attire.

PEDRO: Maldonado, is something wrong?
MALDONADO: Something I find hard to express:
presumptuousness so headstrong;
high estate in lowliness;
and weakness pretending to be strong.

The more this little gypsy is
humbled by her lack of status,
the higher does she set her sights,
aspiring upwards to the heights.
Her behaviour is outrageous.

PEDRO: She does well so leave her be,
don't think less of her and deride

her for it, it pleases me
how with her vanity and pride
she plots and plans her strategy.

What am I? I'm just a churl,
but dream I'm pope, or prince, or earl,
a monarch or an emperor;
so I too fantasise like her
and think I'm lord of all the world.

MALDONADO: With the widow, how'd it go?
PEDRO: All is going wonderfully,
      better than I could have hoped:
      she will give most generously
      or else my name is not Pedro.

      But, tell me, what people are those
      in hunting and fiesta clothes?
MALDONADO: Why, I believe it is the king.
   [Enter the KING and a servant SILERIO and all the hunt.] *
BELICA: Today my desires begin
      to climb love's steep and rocky road.

      To my heart's content I might
      today be set to feast my eyes
      and feed my soul to its delight,
      enjoying the bountiful prize
      that's offered to me by my sight

      and my desires.
MALDONADO: Your great folly
      will end, as far as I can see,
      in an ill that's also great.
BELICA: Oh no, ill can you militate
      against the force of destiny.

   Interval.

*   Cut – the interval meant that the King's entrance was saved for the second half.

After the Interval

The characters that were onstage before the interval are in the same positions and the KING and SILERIO enter.

KING: Tell me, Gypsies, do you know
      if a deer ran past this way?
      It was wounded.

BELICA: Sire, it is so,
      I saw one traverse these plains
      just a little while ago.

      In its right side was buried
      what looked like a sturdy arrow.

KING: It was a piece of lance.

BELICA: If in your entrails perchance
      love's thick iron shaft is carried

      so that the very soul should be
      consumed, it does not help to hide
      or move from place to place or flee.

MALDONADO: I have no doubt this will provide
      proof of her insanity.

KING: Fair gypsy maid, what's that you say?

BELICA: Why Sire, I'd say this if I may:
      love and the hunter are a pair
      due to the harsh nature they share
      and they behave in the same way.

      The beast wounded by the hunter
      although it takes flight terrified
      and runs faster and faster
      still carries the wound in its side
      wherever it may run to.

The heart wounded by Love also
is pierced – by a harpoon of gold –
and he who feels the pang will find
that though he goes out of his mind,
still his passion is in tow.

KING: A gypsy girl who can show
    so much learning is rare to see.
BELICA: I'm a gypsy, well-born though.
KING: Who is your father?
BELICA: Unknown to me!
MALDONADO: Forgive her Sire, she's a lost soul.

    Always raving without basis,
    her head is full of empty spaces
    In spite of her stupidity
    she takes herself so seriously
    and gives herself such airs and graces

    beyond her station.
BELICA: That makes sense!
    It's your own madness makes me so,
    it dwells within your ignorance.
SILERIO· Fortune does smile on you though?
BELICA: Frowns are more in evidence

    at the misfortune of the poor girl
    whose desires grow until
    they burst through clouds in the sky.
SILERIO: So tell me why you aim so high?
BELICA: That's nothing, I'll go higher still.

KING: You have such charm!
BELICA: So much, Señor,
    that trusting in my charms, I raise
    my hopes so high, they fly and soar
    above the air to outer space.

SILERIO: You raise a laugh.

KING: And leave me in awe.

> How curs'd he is who has someone
> whose pleasure stops him having fun.
> Let's go.

SILERIO: At the Queen he aims this dart.

BELICA: Who comes in haste just to depart,
        will not be bless'd by anyone.

The KING and SILERIO exit.

PEDRO: Now look, Belica, it's my guess
        that it would be a big mistake
        to love you, so I think it best
        to take another path and make
        a bid elsewhere for happiness.

> Maldonado the other game
> will be bagged all the same.
> That miserly widow will soon
> be playing a most plentiful tune,
> like the horn of the selfsame name.

> [I'm going to dress up as a hermit
> that my trickery may borrow
> credence from that honest outfit.

MALDONADO: Go and don that strange apparel,
        you know where I said I'd put it.]

PEDRO exits.
Enter THE MASTER OF THE REVELS.

MASTER: Is Maldonado here in person?

MALDONADO: That's me, señor.

MASTER: Give you good day.

BELICA: An officer who's a gentleman?

A wonder! You were never raised
in the village.
MALDONADO: You've got it in one!

Because he's come here from the court.
MASTER: A dance has to be brought
to the palace in the wood.
MALDONADO: More time to practice would be good.
MASTER: I regret the notice is so short.

The king intends to move here from
the monastery where he's been.
MALDONADO: Whatever you say will be done.
BELICA: He's accompanied by the Queen?
MASTER: Who can doubt it, of course she'll come.

BELICA: Is she still prone to jealousy
and severe as she's always been?
MASTER: So they say… Umm I know nothing.
BELICA: Shouldn't it make her more trusting,
being lovely and being Queen?

MASTER: Being in love is sure to rock
even the most lofty mind,
no matter how high its stock.
BELICA: Love and fear are two of a kind
love goes hand in hand with shock.

MASTER: If you already know this, I bet
Love's caught your soul in its net
even though you are so young.
I must go make my rounds among
the villages. Now don't forget,

Maldonado, they're all trying
to arrange dances hereabouts,
so you make sure that your dance shines.

MALDONADO: I'll see that my whole flock's turned out:
    they'll all be dressed up to the nines.

Exeunt.
Enter PEDRO dressed as a hermit with three of four small linen
bags full of sand in his sleeves.

PEDRO: I'm now near the property
    of that lucky widow woman,
    of Marina Sánchez, she
    who guides her soul to heaven
    by means of generosity.

MARINA is listening.

    Now Vicente de Berrocál,
    who's her husband, easily shall
    escape from the terrible blaze
    when his anguish is conveyed
    to Marina. He roasts in hell!

    [And Pedro Benito her son
    straightaway will cease the legion
    of high-pitched screams and moans so dire
    that he is making in the fire
    burning in that blackened region.

    Her nephew, Martínico, he
    with a mole on his face, will be
    leaving behind his grief and gloom,
    seeing that they prepare for him
    the road to majesty and glory.]

MARINA: Wait, I'm coming to you, father!
    If waiting is a chore, I give
    apologies for the bother.
PEDRO: Thanks to heaven is what I give,
    it will smile on me if I bother.

Thanks I give to the one who sent
me into this predicament,
where unafraid of what awaits me
my tongue must extricate me
with honour, gain, and enjoyment.

Oh my memory, please don't fail,
don't let silence by some mishap
make my tongue of no avail.
Convincingly let me play sad
and then let happiness prevail,

help me change my countenance
until this widow gives credence
to all I say to such extent
that in her terror she's content
to be stripped of her affluence.

Enter MARINA.

MARINA: Father let me kiss those feet.
PEDRO: Good countrywoman, don't advance,
       do not touch me. Don't you see
       that homage loses importance
       wherever dwells humility?

       Souls in torment, estranged
       from all comfort, are not assuaged
       by such ceremonies that fill
       the court and won't accept them still,
       even in their greatest pains.

       [One single mass is all they're after,
       more than a thousand 'kiss my hands'.
       This is what I, your Father, have to
       counsel you; courtly gestures can
       only give one cause for laughter.]

       My friend, while I am telling you
       who I am and what I do,

please hold this little sack I've got,
and this other with the tight knot,
they're burdensome and heavy too.

MARINA: Sir I have been told already
who you are and I understand
that you desire covetously
that souls be given compassion
and be not judged rigorously.

I know the honourable task
you've been given and I would ask
that, in conclusion, you tell me,
how my relations' souls may be
granted pardon and may find rest.

PEDRO: Vicente del Berrocál
your husband can, with seventy
escudos as a principal,
claim credit for many good deeds
and clear his slate of sins as well.

Pedro Benito, your poor son,
with forty-six – a tiny sum –
can leave his little oubliette;
with what you give, he will get
joy without comparison.

Your daughter Sancha the Rotund
begs you to answer her plea,
so that with your generous hand
you lower the rope of charity,
to pull her from that deep cavern.

She wants gold escudos as bail –
Fifty-two singles will avail,
or if they're doubles, twenty-six,
this will spring her from that fix
and break the fetters of her jail.

And the direst straits compel
Martín and Quitiera who
are your nephews, to sob and yell
in bitter voices, calling you
from the bottom of a well.

Ten doubloons you're asked to bring –
the two-faced ones – as offerings
on the altars of piety;
these nephews know themselves to be,
among Marina's dearest things.

Your Uncle Sancho Manjón swoons
and suffers in an icy lake
from thirst and cold; he importunes
you with sobs, that you should make
an end to all his misfortunes.

Forty ducats are all he lacks,
you should carefully count the stack
in newly minted silver coin
and I dare boast that I am going
to bear all on my weary back.

MARINA: Señor did you also see there,
my sister Sancha by any chance?
PEDRO: I saw her in a sepulchre
covered by a sheet of bronze,
which is a hard thing, I declare.

She said as I passed over her,
'If you feel pity when you hear
the anguish of the cries I hurl
t'wards you as you go to the world,
tell my sister who's without peer

[that it's up to her entirely
to help me go from these mists
out into shining clarity;

and what will lighten this darkness
is incandescent charity.]

As soon as she has realised
I'm suffering, then she'll provide
thirty florins, and gladly so;
she's like the Good Shepherd, although
you can't pull wool over her eyes.'

[Relying on you for mercy
were all your servants and relations –
they were countless, I saw so many;
two ducats will buy some salvation,
for others you'll pay just a penny.]

And therefore in the final count,
with pen and ink to work it out,
it is my estimation that,
two hundred and fifty ducats
will cover the full amount.

Don't be alarmed that this sack,
the first one I put in your hand
was given to me, if I think back,
by an ogre of a publican,
who told me his daughter, alack,

lies in embers, as in her grave,
and with that sack he hopes to save
her shapely legs from burning, she's
like a heifer of Hercules,
dragged by Cacus to his deep cave.

[It was a mule-driving lad
who gave me the second bag
that I entrusted to your hands
– a traveller in foreign lands,
a good believer though he's bad.]

They're* full of gold from America
mined and panned by the prospector.
With them** the bitterest sorrow,
of souls labouring there below,
will be turned to sweetest nectar.

Therefore, woman so immense,
so good and so very mighty,
let there be nothing that prevents
you relieving the agony
of all these suff'ring penitents.

Undo the knot that disables you
and ties your tongue, so that your true
voice may say with serenity,
'Señor, I'll do what your saintly
sonorous voice tells me to do.'

If the coins of which they spoke
were placed by you in these rough hands,
to those souls' joy, at one fell stroke,
the dreadful fires in those dark lands
will be transformed to wisps of smoke.

And as the sun begins to dip
you might well espy in the air
a soul that's free to stamp and skip,
dancing gracefully up there,
a slave who's now her ladyship.

Where'er you go, where'er you stay,
how they're going to sing your praise
and all around you there will be
souls bowing down in courtesy
because you set them free today.

*   Changed to 'It's' in the RSC production to make sense of the cut paragraph.
** Changed to 'it' in the RSC production to make sense of the cut paragraph.

MARINA gives him back the sacks.

MARINA: Take these, wait a moment for me
　　　　I'm going but I will come back
　　　　with what you want immediately.
She goes.
PEDRO: Heaven will see that you don't lack
　　　　pleasure, rest and tranquillity.

　　　　　　[Clearly here you can descry
　　　　　　the virtuous woman that's sought
　　　　　　in the Bible, whose price is high.
　　　　　　Marina, good fortune be yours,
　　　　　　both in your life and when you die.]

　　　　　　Belilla gypsy girl most fair,
　　　　　　all the fruits of this you'll savour,
　　　　　　without blemish they'll be placed
　　　　　　in your hands, though the flavour
　　　　　　of my suit's not to your taste.

　　　　　　All the money my hoax will net
　　　　　　must be spent on your toilette
　　　　　　and on the dance.　I'd hate to see
　　　　　　that lack of cash and finery
　　　　　　mean your dreams cannot be met.

The WIDOW returns with a bulging cat-purse full of money.

MARINA: Take this, venerable old man,
　　　　there's everything you request,
　　　　I've even put some extra in.
PEDRO: Marina, in giving me this,
　　　　you behave like a true Christian.

　　　　　　Once I'm over that hill I'll sweep
　　　　　　into Rome with just one leap
　　　　　　and to the earth's core with one more,
　　　　　　but now receive my blessing for
　　　　　　I always sow, so others reap.

Healthy teeth is what it fosters
and it prevents you getting lost
when looking at the night-time stars
and stops you being double-crossed
by fraudsters and impostors.

In the faintest heart it will engender
bravery not to surrender
to despair but to stretch its wings
He blesses her.
    because it carries the blessing
    of Pedro the Great Pretender.

He exits.

MARINA: Most trusted man – you who've been sent
    from those souls continually
    toiling and suffering torment –
    since the road to purgatory
    is one that's always in descent,

    be on your way, may you progress
    quickly to the fields of darkness
    or to the vale of bitter tears.
    Discharge your duty with those dear
    coins I gave you in my largess.

    In every escudo there dwells
    my soul that you now take from me –
    and in every penny as well –
    and I'm left here and seem to be,
    like someone put under a spell.

    Now I'm another soul in pain,
    since I see myself estranged
    from the bag I handed over –
    but faith, bear me on your shoulders
    to a more serene domain.

She exits.

Enter SILERIO servant to the King and INÉS the gypsy woman.

SILERIO: Is that girl always aggressive?
INÉS: Yes, Señor, how she gets upset!
　　　　Or angry or happy and yet
　　　　it's over nothing! She's excessive!

　　　　She's ruled by this fantasy,
　　　　which makes us think either in fact,
　　　　or else in her dreams perhaps,
　　　　she belongs to royalty.

　　　　For gypsy men simply won't do
　　　　and she condemns them out of sight.
SILERIO: What we're now giving her to bite
　　　　may well be more than she can chew,

　　　　The King wants to see her, what's more
　　　　he has an amorous intent.
INÉS: In her affections she won't consent
　　　　to be governed by any law.

　　　　But given that in her thoughts
　　　　she's high and mighty she will find
　　　　that for what she has in mind
　　　　a king's not going to fall too short.

　　　　For my part anyway I'll do
　　　　what you've ordered me to do, Sir,
　　　　I'll pass your message on to her,
　　　　not least because it pleases you.

SILERIO: Better to force her to the brink
　　　　than using pleas to exhort her.
INÉS: The horse you drag to the water
　　　　will not necessarily drink.

　　　　Let's have the dance and then let's take
　　　　some time for talking by and by.

The dividends will reach the sky
on this investment we make.

SILERIO: I'll entrust you with something else
that matters more, a caveat.
INÉS: What's the matter?
SILERIO: The secret that,
the Queen is extremely jealous

and the moment she sees a thing
that doesn't please her, she'll make a fuss
which will turn out badly for us
and spoil the pleasure of the King.

INÉS: You should leave, for now I see
our gypsy chief's here.
SILERIO: Of course.
Make sure she gets off her high horse
and you can leave the rest to me.

SILERIO goes.
Enter MALDONADO and PEDRO dressed as the hermit.

PEDRO: It couldn't have been a bigger coup,
if I had scripted every line.
MALDONADO: The greatest trickster of our time
must offer up his crown to you.

With ingenuity and guile,
you size things up and carry through.
I have to say my name for you
is Swindler of the Cunning Wiles.

Free of censure and dishonour,
you emerge on each occasion
for in your heart's a double agent
and in your tongue's an orator.

INÉS: The King expects this afternoon,
     my chief, to see our dance displayed.
PEDRO: That's when Belica may parade,
     all my riches and good fortune.

     Let her clean herself up and throw
     on every scrap of finery.
INÉS: Perhaps you forge her destiny
     in what you do, renown'd Pedro.

     We must rehearse; the King can't wait,
     and let's make sure that we impress
     everyone there with our dress.
PEDRO: Yes, let's go, we're already late.

   They all exit.
   Enter the KING and SILERIO.

SILERIO: I say she'll be here presently
     she's coming with the dancers, Sire.
KING: How it increases, my desire!
     It's demanding more of me

     than I thought, I'm out of control!
     I blame them for not being here;
     it's tiring when hope is near
     and your expectations grow.

     And you'll hide it from the Queen's eyes.
SILERIO: I'll do whatever pleases you.
KING: The gypsy's dance will please me too
     tell the girl that then improvise,

     so that she can clearly see
     that my desire is unconfined.
SILERIO: If love was ever of sound mind,
     I'd think that this were lunacy.

     I will neither absolve nor blame
     since lovers' minds court confusion.

KING: I'm to blame, need absolution,
    though this confession's rather lame

    and comes too late.
SILERIO: The Queen's coming.
KING: You must keep your wits about you,
    my cause will be lost without you,
    be prepared for anything,

    for this jealous woman, sad to say,
    has eyes sharper than a lynx.
SILERIO: You'll enjoy the charms, methinks,
    of that fair gypsy girl today.

  Enter the QUEEN.

QUEEN: Sire, you came without me? What?
    You prefer us to be apart?
KING: This solitude gladdens the heart;
    it's such a fresh and lovely spot!

QUEEN: And my company annoys and tires?
KING: Please don't say that, it's a lie!
    I thank my stars when you're nearby
    for the joy your presence inspires.

QUEEN: Anything brings dread upon me,
    inflames me, my desires increase
    If I can't see you or at least,
    if your shadow falls not on me.

    Though I act impertinently,
    if you accept that love's my Sire,
    and that I'm ruled by his empire,
    then you'll bear with me patiently.

SILERIO: Here come the dancers, Sire and Ma'am,
    if my ears are to be believed.

KING: So let's watch them, by your leave,
   sitting here amidst the charms

   offered by the flowers, the roses
   that make this a delightful spot.
QUEEN: Very well.
  Enter CRESPO the Mayor and TARUGO the alderman.
CRESPO: I'll speak to him! Why not?
   You don't understand the proooo!

   I declare I'm going to complain
   to the King for this impotence.
TARUGO: Well, Crespo, here's his reverence
   right here.
CRESPO: Is this a trick you're playing?

   Which one?
KING: This one. What has been done
   to you good man?
CRESPO: What can I say?
   Our dance is put in disarray
   by your pages who've made fun

   of my efforts, I'd like to see
   them punished by the worst ordeal
   I can't ejaculate how I feel –
   it's about as bad as it could be.

   Twenty-four young lads as lasses
   all salt of the earth and hulking,
   came to… I don't know why the king
   won't give you two thousand lashes,

   pages! You must be the worst scum
   that the entire world ever saw!
   As I was saying, I gave my all –
   and my all is a tidy sum –

   to gather these missy misters
   together – I'm the Mayor you see –

to entertain Your Majesty,
with their little bells and whiskers.

I didn't want to bring maidens,
they're used so often that they bore,
but rather a beguiling corps
of their tinkling male relations,

smart and swanky as is the use.
But when your pages, Your Highness,
saw them got up in this dress
I swear to you, all hell broke loose.

With whips made out of rags and dirt
they gave out such beatings that soon
my entire dancing platoon,
had to retreat destroyed and hurt.

They've manhandled – these upstarts! –
a supreme dancing company,
for never did a Prince or Lord see
a better one around these parts.

QUEEN: Bring them back together then.
     The king will wait, I'll make sure of that.

TARUGO: Even if some want to come back
     they won't be able to dance again.

     They were so liberally supplied
     with punches, slaps and drubbings,
     beaten to a pulp with clubbings,
     that each of them has a tanned hide.

QUEEN: It would be so fascinating
     to see. Can't you bring us just one?
TARUGO: I'll go and see what can be done.
CRESPO: Remember that the King is waiting,

     Tarugo, fetch here from the troupe,
     if he's not limping too badly,

> as when I last saw him sadly,
> my nephew, Diego-Fly-The-Coop.

TARUGO exits.

> He'll shed some illumination
> on how the rest would have appeared.
> Oh how many pages are reared
> at court and brought to damnation!

> Given they're pages to the King
> and all of them are so well born,
> then their behaviour, I'd have sworn,
> should show more control and breeding.

> Their actions are so base and low,
> that four student faculties,
> within four universities,
> don't hold the vice your pages know.

> And their behaviour imparts,
> that by giving us such knocks,
> though they wear crosses on their smocks,
> they carry devils in their hearts.

TARUGO returns bringing with him DIEGO-FLY-THE-COOP, wearing 'papos' (headgear that is twisted over the ears), a green baize skirt decorated with yellow, cut at the knee, and in leggings with bells, a tightly corseted garment or blouse with padded chest; and although he may play the drum, he remains stock still.

TARUGO: Here, Crespo, I've found your nephew.
      Behold!
CRESPO: Play, Pingalong, quickly,
      that Her Good Majesty may see
      all the trouble we've gone to,

He plays.

> and how novel's our ambition.
> Come on, you idiot, move your arse!

Or at least bow before you start
and beg them for their permission!

[Hello! Nephew! You stupid cuss!
Dance a little! Can you hear me?
TARUGO: Well, as far as I can see,
the devil's making fools of us.]

Straighten up, you useless clown!
He prods him.
CRESPO: Satanic pages, curse you all!
QUEEN: Stop hitting him and ask no more!
CRESPO: Your obstinacy casts us down

into the depths.
DIEGO: God only knows
I can't move – for Jesus' sake!
SILERIO: What a tender lassie you make.
TARUGO: Why?
DIEGO: I've broken one of the toes

on my right foot.
KING: Then leave him be.
Find your village, go back there!
CRESPO: It's quite near here – where I am mayor –
in case you want to reward me.

Make each page pay the penalty
and we'll bring you another dance
which, in costume and performance,
will reach the heights of novelty.

Exit TARUGO, CRESPO and DIEGO FLY THE COOP.

QUEEN: That Mayor is just the limit.
KING: And the dancer was so well dressed.
QUEEN: The argument so well expressed,
if there's a prize he should win it.

SILERIO: But now here comes another dance,
      it's the gypsy maidens.
QUEEN: Oh yes,
      they're always so smart in their dress,
      and lovely in their appearance.

KING: It's so belittling for a king
      to be fearful of a gypsy.
SILERIO: Amongst these girls, Your Majesty,
      you'll see one, who's most striking,

      her beauty is breathtaking
      and she's as honest as she's fair.
KING: It costs me dear to look at her.
QUEEN: Where are they? Why are we waiting?

*Enter the MUSICIANS, dressed as gypsies; INÉS and BELICA
and another two* gypsy girls in their best costumes – especially
BELICA who has to outshine the rest. Enter also PEDRO as a
gypsy and MALDONADO. [They have rehearsed two dance
movements and carry tambors/side drums.]*

PEDRO: May God preserve Your Majesties,
      we, your humble gypsies, today
      will give a stunning display
      of brio and vivacity.

      Oh that this dance might be enhanced
      by brocade which we could parade
      before you, but we are stayed
      by limited means, which means our dance

      is lowlier, but Belilla,
      all the same, with her grace, her face
      and her eyes will leave no trace
      of vexations and replace them here

*   The RSC production used all five actresses in the cast.

with pleasure and wonder for you,
God's gypsy girls, begin! Be fleet
of foot!

QUEEN: How this gypsy can speak!

MALDONADO: Dance at the front, the two of you!

PEDRO: Ya Belica, my April flower
       and Inés, the power and lustre
       of your illustrious dancing
       will muster fame for this dance of ours!

They dance.

       Let the dance be fleet Ginesa!
       [Don't falter, don't alter the beat!
       Look Francisquilla how your feet
       defeat you! Ay! Bless her!

MALDONADO: They make the cross wide and long,
       it's as if their arms take flight.
       This dance is heavenly alright
       or I'm an ass with its saddle on.

PEDRO: Ya, darting wagtails give chase!
       And you chirping sandpipers, fly!
       Carry your bodies with pride;
       lift your arms to the sky with grace!

MALDONADO: With guitars sounding in your ears
       make quicksilver of your feet.

PEDRO: Holy – ! They're doing well those three!

MALDONADO: All five of them deserve our cheers.

       But Belica's unparalleled –
       the grace and brio she displays!]
       BELICA falls next to/against the KING.

KING: It's only right that I should raise
     this eighth new wonder of the world.

     And know that you receive from me,
     with my hand, my soul as well.

QUEEN: Oh, this girl has done very well
     and the King behaved so gallantly.

     How well he did to lower
     his majesty by kneeling down
     only to raise up from the ground
     a fallen gypsy girl like her!

BELICA: In this he showed nobility,
     for it would be irreverence
     if anyone in his presence,
     should be abased or lowly.

     His greatness was not disgraced
     by this in any way at all
     because majesty that's assured
     cannot ever be debased.

     And it may be my destiny
     in a strange way, as I see things,
     that I should be treated by kings
     with gallantry.

QUEEN: So I can see.

     It's a privilege that pertains
     to beauty.

KING: Madam, I petition
     you, don't spoil the exhibition;
     it makes us gay and entertains.

QUEEN: How these words so lightly stated
     grip my heart, bring me dismay.
     Take these gypsy girls away
     and let them be incarcerated!

For such is beauty's tyranny,
it gets its power from being seen
and conquers any heart in sight.
KING: Are you jealous of a gypsy?

That really is most disgusting,
an insufferable thing to say!
QUEEN: I'd agree with what *you* say,
if you behaved like a true king

or if she had just a fraction
less beauty, but it's not so.
Away with them to prison! Go!
SILERIO: That's a very strange reaction.

INÉS: Don't let this jealous thought of yours
disturb you, Ma'am, in this fashion,
nor make you do things that are rash an'
that really don't have any cause.

You only need to hear the tale
I'll tell you in private somewhere –
and this is no attempt, I swear,
to talk myself out of your jail.

QUEEN: To my chambers without ado,
be sure to bring them after me.
The QUEEN and the GYPSY WOMEN go.
KING: Seldom does one see jealousy
that doesn't smack of cruelty too.

SILERIO: I have a nasty feeling, Sire,
arising from what happened there.
You see, I made this gypsy aware
of the extent of your desire.

She has some secret to convey
to the Queen – my apprehension
is, now knowing your intention,
she's going to give the game away.

KING: In the bitterness of my woe
      there's nothing left for me to fear,
      I've reached rock bottom, my nadir,
      I'm as low as I can go.

      Come on, it remains to be seen,
      how we'll find a way to temper
      the confused, angry distemper
      that is governing the Queen.

  Exit the KING and SILERIO.

PEDRO: Well, it cannot be denied
      we made a hash of that business.
MALDONADO: What a disaster! I confess
      it's left me feeling stupefied.

      Belica arrested! Inés
      conversing with the Queen like that!
      It gives me much to wonder at!
PEDRO: And even more to fear.
MALDONADO: Yes, yes.

PEDRO: I'm not waiting, I'm afraid,
      for the outcome, I'm going to beat
      an extremely hasty retreat
      from this gypsy escapade.

      An ecclesiastical cap
      and the reverent arm of the Church
      will help me out of this lurch,
      I don't intend to take the rap.

      Goodbye Maldonado!
MALDONADO: Not so fast!
      What will you do?
PEDRO: Nothing at all.
      I'm sorry I don't have the gall.
      As I see it, the die is cast.

Nothing is going to keep me here,
not rope for galleys or for gallows,

MALDONADO: You'd let yourself drown in such shallows?
I'd never thought you'd show such fear;

I never thought you'd run away
from the battle, that you were made
of sterner stuff.

PEDRO: But my brigade
will live to fight another day.

Though you don't really know me yet,
Maldonado, you have to see,
an honourable man should be
not daring but circumspect.

To foresee danger's to be wise.
So rest in peace, I'm on my way.

MALDONADO: Your fears are groundless; however, you may
please yourself.

PEDRO: I just recognize

there are many grounds here for fears
and, as their power is supreme,
the fury of a king and queen
goes beyond all laws and frontiers.

MALDONADO: If that's the case then we should go,
it seems it would be well advised.

MUSICIANS: All of us are petrified,
Maldonado.

MALDONADO: Alright, I know.

Exeunt.

End of the Second Act.

ACT THREE

Enter the QUEEN, carrying some jewels in a handkerchief, with MARCELO, an elderly gentleman.

QUEEN: Marcelo, I beg you answer me
    unless thereby you'd jeopardise
    both your honour and your life
    because you're sworn to secrecy.

MARCELO: Ask any questions you desire.
    At your feet, Ma'am, I proclaim,
    I lay my life and my good name.
    Serving you is all I require.

QUEEN: Who owns these valuable gems?
    To whom did they belong before?
MARCELO: The man who was and is my lord
    once had ownership of them.

QUEEN: How were they appropriated?
    It's very important to me
    to find out how this came to be,
    were they stolen or donated?

MARCELO: Given that the earth now covers
    both the crime and the dishonour –
    if that which honest love has forged
    can be called crime and dishonour –
    I intend to break a silence,
    that is important no longer
    to the living nor to the dead,
    yet it's an important matter
    to all. One night when light was scarce
    and darkness was abundant
    I was standing on the terrace
    hoping against hope to see her

whom, you, my Lady, gave to me
to be my wife and partner,
when in a troubled whisper
the Duchess Felix Alva –
may she dwell with God in glory –
called out to me in great distress
'Whoever you may be, Señor,
may fortune give you just reward
by fulfilling your desires,
if you show Christian charity
by helping one in dire need
who calls out to you for succour.
Take this most noble treasure
that fortune doesn't favour,
and, giving her a name you choose,
baptise her with holy water.'
She was lowering a basket
of white and scented wicker
on a braid of her hair that served
as a kind of rope for her.
Saying no more, she went inside.
I was left at this juncture
duty-bound and disconcerted,
full of foreboding and wonder,
for in the basket I could hear
the cries of some creature
which sounded like a newborn babe's.
What a juncture! What a duty!
In the end, that you may gather
how this tale ends without delay,
I'll say that with great diligence,
I left the city straight away
and went to the village that lies
beyond that hill, purely because
it was near. Heaven however
leavens all our misfortunes.
With Aurora's rosy finger

it pointed out a gypsy camp
it had placed there in my path where
I found some humble dwellings.
After some negotiations
she was taken into the care
of an aging gypsy woman,
who set about unwrapping her
and found among the swaddling clothes,
tied in a linen cloth, those gems.
Immediately I recognised them
as belonging to my master,
your brother Lord Rosamiro.
I left them with that little girl
who came to me in that basket –
no child could have been lovelier.
I charged the old gypsy woman
to raise her and baptise her
and dress her in humble but clean
clothing. Nothing could be stranger
when my tongue gave its account
of these events to your brother.
He said to me: 'Marcelo
just like the jewels the child is mine
and the Duchess Felix Alva –
the glory for whom I suffer,
who alone is the object of
my desires – she's her mother.
The birth may have been premature,
the handing over ill-prepared,
but all the same this can't eclipse
her brilliant handling of this matter.'
As we conversed, the bells began
to toll in a mournful manner
and every single monastery
and parish joined the clamour.
The sad ringing was so widespread
that we could only infer

that this tribute was returning
someone high-ranking to the earth.
Entering at this sad moment
a page clarified the matter,
saying, 'Alas, my Lord, she's dead,
my lady Felix Alva.
She died most unexpectedly
last night, Señor, and so that's why
so many bells are ringing out
and so many people cry.'
When he heard this news
he remained there in a stupor,
his eyes were fixed and didn't move,
nor did his body either.
But then he came back to himself
but not a word did he utter
except to say, 'Have the child raised,
don't take the jewels away from her;
she'll be brought up as a gypsy
and she should not be made aware
of who she is as she grows up.
That's my wish in this affair.'
In two hours he left for the frontiers
and there the Moors were diminished
by his spear, and his happiness
diminished by his memories.
He always writes to me and asks
that I should visit Belica –
thus had the wise gypsy named her
who so lovingly had raised her.
[I cannot understand his purpose,
what his aim is, why he wishes
not to have this story known
that is so sad, so singular.]
They have said to the young lady
that a gypsy robber stole her
and she believes herself to be

some royal personage's daughter.
She's done and said a thousand things
the many times I have seen her
to make you easily believe
that she wears a crown already.
The woman who had nursed her died
and, with the jewels, entrusted her
to the care of her own daughter,
who's just as young if not as fair.
This young woman had these jewels
but knows no more about her
than her mother knew before her,
ignorant of the provenance
and the parentage of Isabél,
the very ladylike and fair,
the very discreet and fiery,
that very lovely maid, your niece.
That's my answer to your question
about these jewels, whether they were
freely given or were stolen.
Now I'm surprised to see them there.

QUEEN: I am familiar with half
of this remarkable saga
and there is no discrepancy
in either account that I've heard.
If you should happen to see her,
tell me would you recognise her,
this lovely gypsy girl?

MARCELO: Of course;
as I would myself, Señora.

QUEEN: Well then, wait here a little while.

Exit the QUEEN.

MARCELO: Who was it brought these jewels here?
There's nothing that can be concealed
from heaven or time forever.
Was my revelation wrong?

> Yes; a hasty tongue that affords
> no room for reasoning and thought,
> brings condemnation not rewards.

The QUEEN returns with BELICA and INÉS.

QUEEN: Is this the man who came to see
    your sister?
INÉS: Yes, I can state
    that I saw him communicate
    with my mother frequently.

QUEEN: Given that and her resemblance
    to my brother, then I can see,
    that the face I have before me
    is my niece's countenance.

MARCELO: You can safely believe that for
    she whose hand you hold's no other
    than the treasure that your brother
    loves and will love forever more.

> If on earth God's distinguished her
> through her father, then no less
> has heaven rendered her peerless
> through her mother who resides there

> and she herself, through her beauty,
> deserves to be held in esteem.

Enter the KING with the GENTLEMAN

KING: It's a proven fact, it would seem,
    jealousy goes with insanity.

QUEEN: And with love too, My Lord, a fact
    that you forgot to mention.
KING: Jealousy is rage and dissension
    and love is always free of that.

> When the cause is good, assuredly
> no ill effects can come from it.

99

QUEEN: With me it's quite the opposite,
    I'm tormented by jealousy

    which never fails to pursue me –
    it's born of my love for you.
KING: The fact that it's deluding you
    will avenge the wrong you do me.

    Through your questions, you have cited
    your suspicions with vehemence,
    but you have no evidence
    by which I may be indicted.

    And neither am I so depraved –
    you'd see it if you'd just reflect –
    that I'd incline my royal neck
    before a humble gypsy maid.

QUEEN: Reflect on this, Sire, she is fair
    and even the most mighty
    and the highest majesty
    is vanquished by beauty so rare.

    If only through my eyes you could heed
    the beauty of her lovely eyes.
KING: If you hope to antagonise
    me, you're not going to succeed.

QUEEN: What? It makes your anger increase
    to look at such a young lady,
    who, as well as being lovely,
    also aspires to be my niece?

BELICA: Inés, what is all this about?
    I can't help feeling that maybe
    they're all making fun of me.
INÉS: Keep quiet, then you'll soon find out.

QUEEN: If, with a mind free of trouble,
    you look at her, whom do you see?

KING: If I trust what my eyes tell me,
    she is Rosamiro's double.

QUEEN: Not surprising! She's his daughter,
    you should treat her accordingly.
GENTLEMAN: Are you joking, Your Majesty?
QUEEN: That assumption would distort a

    truth that is simply obvious.
KING: If you're not joking, then it's apt
    for me to be completely rapt
    on hearing such news as this.

QUEEN: Come, Isabél, approach the king,
    take his hand, tell him he ought to
    greet you as my brother's daughter.
BELICA: As one in thrall I come to him.

KING: You lovely child get up, of course
    I really ought to have suspected
    that better fortune's to be expected
    from such lovely looks as yours.

    But tell me, Madame, how befell it
    that you came to know this story?
QUEEN: Although it's short and extraordinary,
    now is not the time to tell it.

    To the city without ado!
    On the way I'll tell you about
    all that's happened, you'll not doubt
    that every word of this is true.

KING: Let's go.
MARCELO: Sire, it's definite,
    this tale you've heard is not a lie,
    her looks confirm it, so do I
    who had a major part in it.

As they make their exit. INÉS and BELICA stay behind for a moment.

INÉS: Belica, now you're off to be
     a niece to Her Royal Highness,
     condescend to let your eyes rest
     on us in our humility.

     You must remember, more than once
     we two went on a stealing spree
     and without any rivalry
     we danced together more than twice.

     Although often at odds with you
     and you with me, in retrospect
     I always have had great respect
     and fear for you – I showed it too!

     Now it's in your power to do
     something good for us poor gypsies
     and thus you will surpass those ladies
     born much luckier than you.

     Your response ought to befit,
     the importance of your standing.
BELICA: Then give me a memorandum
     and I will try to deal with it.

Exeunt.
Enter PEDRO with (ecclesiastical) cloak and cap as a student

PEDRO: It is said that variety
     is a spice that makes the world
     more pleasant and more beautiful,
     a thing that's clear for all to see.

     Eating the same dish is cloying,
     if the same object's always placed
     before the eyes of one with taste,
     it is irksome and annoying.

It's tiring if you're always dressed
in the same outfit. For change lifts
your spirits, your perspective shifts,
that's why it's as good as a rest.

I'll leave this world a success,
when God comes to take me away,
because I'll be able to say
I was a second Proteus.

[May God help me, what a parade
of costumes and occupations,
and what varied operations,
what exquisite speeches I've made.]

In student garb now I'm an outlaw
and flee the Queen in great unease,
fearing all the calamities
that fickle fate may have in store.

But why do I complain that luck's
been very changeable with me
if our soul should always be
in a continual state of flux?

So let God send me where I may
be able to serve him well.

Enter a FARMER with two hens.

FARMER: I couldn't sell them, you can tell
     that it's a black Tuesday today.

PEDRO: Come here, brother, and let me see
     Closer! What is bothering you?
     These are birds of great quality
     and in each of them there shines through
     your enormous charity.

     Go with God and abnegate them,
     and from afar adulate them,
     as holy relics celebrate them,

in bucolic rites dedicate them
to sacrifice and venerate them.

FARMER: Do whatever satisfies you
as long as you don't falter
in paying me, turn them into
relics or make them an altar.
PEDRO: The only payment for these two

which would be both just and holy
is using them to satisfy
the most respected Christian's dreams.
FARMER: Señor Blockhead, all your schemes
will be in vain however fly.

Enter two PLAYERS.

PEDRO: You're a hypocrite and evil too,
for you are not affording me
the consideration that's due
to a man who's far too worthy
to be playing tricks on you,

a man who fully intends
to pay a ransom with these hens
to free two captives in Algiers,
alive and well, so it appears,
through divine Grace that God extends.

PLAYER: This story really is a beauty
and this kind of seminarist
plays holy brother to the T.
PEDRO: The power of self-interest!
It's so brutal and miserly!

How is it you try to eschew –
and for such paltry trifles too –
setting free these Christian souls
from the hands of barbaric foes?
May cannibals devour you!

FARMER: Señor Featherbrain, please say,
    if, in the name of all that's bless'd,
    my hens are perhaps scrawny strays,
    so that, though they're all I possess,
    I'd willingly give them away?

    Let the rich rescue these Christians,
    or courtiers or courtesans,
    let alms-givers and friars be asked,
    for I don't have that kind of cash,
    just what I've earned with my two hands.

PLAYER: Let's help this little hoax along.
    You are a very thoughtless man
    a good-for-nothing vagabond;
    you're so soulless that nothing can
    move you or make you respond.

PEDRO: May the curse of my fox's fell
    and of my cap and gown as well,
    fall on you and all your kind
    and may I see you confined
    in Algiers in a prison cell,

    to see how you enjoy it when
    some so and so will not consent
    for just two measly little hens –
    Oh hearts of bronze that won't be bent!
    Oh Satanic holding pens!

    [Oh what a life of misery!
    Reduced to such straits! We see
    gentlemen come to such a pass,
    they beg from folk of lower class,
    the damned and the unholy.]

FARMER: Bloody hell! Give me back my hens
    I'm not a man for almsgiving

PLAYER: How little you comprehend
　　　　the trials involved in ransoming
　　　　two plump and weighty gentlemen!

　　　　And I picture them to be
　　　　bearded men and most portly,
　　　　their build and presence inspires awe,
　　　　and they seem to be worth much more
　　　　than three hundred ducats to me.

　　　　I want to free them from their yokes
　　　　using just two hens as ransom.
　　　　The heart of this ignorant bloke
　　　　who grew up here amongst the oaks
　　　　is so evil and so loathsome!

　　　　These wicked people will not budge
　　　　from bearing malice and a grudge,
　　　　they're so miserly and greedy.
FARMER: I can't win, you three play jury,
　　　　executioner and judge.

　　He exits.

PEDRO: He got off lightly if he only knew it.
PLAYER: Leave him m'lud, don't pursue it.
　　　　He's left his hens here anyhow.
PLAYER: So what are we going to do now?
PEDRO: Say what you want and we'll do it.

　　　　First let's pluck our ransom, then,
　　　　to close the case and to sum up,
　　　　we'll see if there's some drinking den
　　　　or hostelry where we can sup
　　　　and indulge ourselves, gentlemen.

　　　　For I seriously intend
　　　　to supply henceforth as your friend
　　　　all trimmings that could be desired.

PLAYER: There's one big snag – we're required
      at rehearsals! We must attend!

PEDRO: Rehearsals? You mean you're actors?
PLAYER: I'm afraid we are for our sins.
PEDRO: Make my good luck and all my riches
      higher than the Atlas mountains,
      make this pygmy a colossus!

      What you two represent to me
      is to the very nth degree
      everything that I most crave.
PLAYER: What typhoon blows to make you rave
      and whip away your sanity?

PEDRO: My life must be an actor's one
      so that my admiring fans
      will sing of the things I've done
      till they're recounted in the lands
      of the rising and the setting sun.

      My fame will fly on the breeze
      to infernos deeper than Dante's.
      I'm changing what I'm called as well
      my Christian name will be Miguel
      and as surname I'll take Cervantes.

      [This was my master's name, you see,
      the one who helped me recognise
      how very cruel this world can be;
      that blind man who didn't need eyes
      to see the world's duplicity.]

      My name will be on the agenda
      in halls where folk dress in splendour
      and shacks where they've coarse linen on
      and I consign to oblivion
      the name Pedro the Great Pretender.

PLAYER: Sir it's gibberish what you say.
    We can't make head or tail of it.
PEDRO: To tell my story would betray
    a lack of wit – to make you sit
    and hear it now would anyway.

    You'd get a numb posterior.
    But if my luck's superior
    as an actor, then you'll be
    witness to the ingenuity
    that dwells in my interior.

    You'll notice my aptitude first
    and foremost in an interlude
    I'll play a ruse for all it's worth.
Enter another PLAYER.
PLAYER: You've not noticed, I conclude,
    that it's high time that we rehearsed?

    The King has asked to see a play,
    you've caused an hour and half's delay,
    the director's waiting, shame on you!
PLAYER: To put things right all we must do
    is go and find him straightaway.

    So come on good man, don't linger,
    you'll be an actor on the spot.
PEDRO: I'll show you, I won't malinger!
    I'll make a director too with what
    I know in my little finger.

    Now I think the time is nigh
    for the prediction spoken by
    that fortune-telling seer
    about my future and career,
    to be fulfilled and verified.

    Now I can be student or pope,
    a patriarch or a king,

wear a crown or wear a cope,
for every rank and every calling
come within an actor's scope;

and though the life can be a grind,
it's one for an enquiring mind
because it deals with new ideas.
Even a detractor who sneers,
won't say it's of an idle kind.

Enter a DIRECTOR with some sheets of paper indicating a play
script.

DIRECTOR: Gentlemen I can't forgive you,
you're taking such a liberty!
I can see I'm going to be
forced to lose my patience with you.

You see how unlucky I am?
You would have thought that twenty days
was enough time to stage this play.
I think you just don't give a damn!

What's annoying, here's the rub –
God, it does incur my wrath –
not one of you ever takes off
when it's time to eat your grub.

But for rehearsals, isn't it funny,
though we send dogs and ferrets out
and even the town criers shout,
you can't be found for love nor money?

PEDRO: To play someone sharp as can be,
who's well-versed in the con-man's art,
I'm the man for such a part,
I've got the patter, just ask me.

DIRECTOR: He seems suitable enough
if this is not an idle boast.

PEDRO: I understand what matters most.
for an actor. I know my stuff.*

Enter the MASTER OF REVELS

MASTER: Even now they're still so slow?
Must I wait until they choose
to come? Have they not heard the news
that all the palace seems to know?

They make my vexation increase
with their dawdling. Just get cracking!
They're expected by the king,
and by the Queen and her new niece.

DIRECTOR: What niece?

MASTER: A gypsy, who as they say,
is an extremely lovely maid.

PEDRO: (*Aside.*) This is Belica, I'm afraid.
(*To the MASTER.*) Is this news true?

MASTER: It's clear as day.

You just couldn't come upon a
greater truth as far as I know,
what's more the Queen desires to throw
a fiesta in her honour.

Come with me and then you can
see what happens on the spot.

PEDRO: It would advantage me a lot,
if you would let me join your band.

DIRECTOR: Come on, later we'll conclude
this discussion, now let's test
your skill in you new interest,
by rehearsing an interlude.

---

*   The rest of this speech (beginning 'The skills that are prerequisite') was
transposed in the RSC production to the end of the play.

PEDRO: There will not be any body,
    who is able to surpass me.
MASTER: Gentlemen it's late already.
DIRECTOR: Anyone missing?
PLAYER: Nobody.

They all go.
Enter the KING and SILERIO.

KING: Always her beauty shines through,
    in any dress she's fair to me,
    as a gypsy girl she slew me,
    as a lady, she's learning to.

    And my desire is not made less
    because we're related; rather,
    with an even greater ardour
    my whole soul is in distress.

Enter the MUSICIANS – guitars play.

    But what can that music be?
SILERIO: It's the actors I presume
    on their way to the dressing room.
KING: This fiesta's depressing me;

    I just want to commune alone
    with my desires, then I'll be free
    to brave the waves of this wild sea
    of love into which I've been thrown.*

    Hark, can you hear what's being sung?
    It's my story, that's a sign
    it will live on in people's minds
    for many centuries to come.

---

*   The song was sung at this point by two of the PLAYERS.

MUSICIANS*: *The gypsies are dancing*
they're watched by the King
the Queen she is jealous
and sends them to jail.

Just like the magi who
brought gifts to the King,
Inés and Belica
brought gypsy dancing.
Belica is nervous,
falls close to the King;
the King is so courtly,
gives her his hand.
But lovely Belica,
because she's so fair,
it makes the Queen jealous
she sends them to jail.

SILERIO: Their minds are so engrossed that they
don't even notice we are here.

KING: And their song shows, it would appear,
how the senses get carried away.

MUSICIAN 1: The King is here, we'd better shush.
Our song may not be agreeable
to him.

MUSICIAN 2: But of course it will!
It's original and fresh

and it doesn't make any claim
that's not serious and poignant too,
which everybody knows is true,
that the Queen's a jealous dame.

It's in the nature of a wife
to be jealous of her husband.

---

*   See Appendix for lyrics used in the RSC production.

KING: What a most insightful man!
    Go to hell with your insight.

    Silerio what shall I do?
    Side by side come my life and death.
SILERIO: To both of them show faithfulness,
    on one hand feigned, the other true.

*Enter the QUEEN and BELICA now dressed as a lady; INÉS
as a gypsy; MALDONADO, the DIRECTOR, MARTÍN CRESPO
the Mayor and PEDRO THE GREAT PRETENDER.*

PEDRO: Famed Isabél, you're now elite,
    who were Belica not long ago,
    the trickster of renown, Pedro
    prostrates himself here at your feet.

    He's giving up pranks and he's
    decided to change his great name
    from Pretender to gain more fame –
    to Miguel de Cervantes.

    [In front of you is the former
    gypsy whom you knew as Pedro,
    who has been converted though,
    into a renowned performer.]

    He'll shower you with plays, mistress,
    you won't have seen the like before,
    but now that you're no longer poor
    maybe you just won't care less.

    Your pretension and my own
    may be now fulfilled conclusively:
    mine through fiction exclusively,
    yours because the truth is known.

    Cruel tricks or harmless jokes reveal
    fate works in many different ways,

making joke lords who jest in plays,
or true ladies whose words are real.

I an actor shall be a king
when I perform one in a scene;
you, watching me, are half a queen,
by your worth and by your breeding.

I'll serve you in jest and joke,
you can grant me a boon for real,
if you're not ungrateful and reveal
yourself to be like common folk.

[For if ever someone should be
elevated from rags to riches,
always one fact remains, which is
that their beginnings were lowly.

But your nature and virtue attest
that I can say with certitude,
no shadow of ingratitude
will ever fall upon your breast.]

I, who have such faith, implore you,
most eminent niece of the Queen,
given he who for you has been
a gypsy now bows before you

to broach with the king a topic,
something which I dearly wish –
no opportunism in this –
I'm simply being philanthropic.

KING: I will grant your wish right here
     if you tell me what you require.
PEDRO: Because it's right, what I desire,
     I'll ask it without any fear.

And it is this: since it is plain,
that an actor's art only tries

to instruct through its exercise
and of course to entertain,

that great skill and commitment,
and endless curiosity,
and knowing when to be thrifty
and when to be extravagant;

all are needed, let no-one do it
who does not have the qualities
that this profession clearly needs,
to instruct and delight through it.

To find the person most fitting
to be director, let's see a show
of his performed, so no arsehole
can get the job through bullshitting.

And they'll take pains in how they do
their job if this is understood:
a profession's only as good,
as the aim it aspires to.

BELICA: I will see that your petition
      earns a concession from the King.
KING: To you I'll concede anything,
      favours for him or commissions!

QUEEN: And I regard with different eyes
      the way you are regarding her,
      and everything you do for her
      brings joy, not a nasty surprise.

So I'm inclined to make my peace,
and make this promise too:
between my jealousy and you
is interposed her being my niece.

So let's enjoy this comedy
and thank heaven it's not ordained,

that my jealousy should have changed
the play into a tragedy.

Straightaway I must impart
to my brother what has happened.
She exits.

KING: I can touch her with my hand
and she's here now in my heart.

Imagination sets its sights
on the least possible of things,
if in their hopes even kings
aspire to impossible heights.

SILERIO: This kinship's not so all denying
or so close that we won't at last
find a way out of this impasse.

KING: But in the meantime I am dying.

Exit the KING and SILERIO.

MALDONADO: Lady Belica, hello there;
It's Maldonado, won't you wait?
Your gypsy chief –

BELICA: My high estate
requires that I should be elsewhere.

Pardon me please Maldonado
I'll talk to you some other day.

INÉS: Belica, my sister, may –

BELICA: The Queen is waiting I must go.

Exit BELICA.

INÉS: Exit Belica! I'm scandalised.
Who'd have thought this two days ago!
I'd not believe she'd behave so
if I'd not seen it with my eyes.

So help me God, what ingratitude
and what a surly girl she is.

PEDRO: So much we hold for certain is
destroyed by life's vicissitudes;

[they bring so many calumnies
and prize what was ill-begotten,
so that in one hour is forgotten,
what was learnt over centuries.

CRESPO: Pedro! Here? Dressed up! How come?
Just what have you done to yourself?

PEDRO: If I'd not looked after myself
I fear I might have been undone!

I've changed my name and job of late,
For I've set my store merely on
becoming a chameleon.*

CRESPO: My man, you always have been great.

I've come to collect the prize
for the dance you advocated,
in which you clearly defecated
wherein your ingenuity lies.

I'm sure the fame it would have won –
if there was no such thing as pages –
would have lasted down the ages
until the very final one.

Clemente and Clemency
have no misfortunes and are well,
and Benita and her Pascual
are getting along handsomely.]

---

*   Or more accurately:

From now on I will appear a
monster of nature, a chimera.

Enter the DIRECTOR.

DIRECTOR*: So now you've gained admission
        to this happy trade of ours,
        because your rare mental powers
        deserve greater recognition.

PEDRO: The skills that are prerequisite
        and that an actor must possess
        in order to have some success
        are as rare as they're infinite.

        The first is a good memory;
        the second is a fluent tongue;
        third: in his wardrobe should be hung
        a fair amount of finery.

        A good figure is *de rigueur*
        when he's playing the young heroes,
        in speech he can't be grandiose,
        nor affected in his gesture.

        He'll act with studied carelessness
        the grave old man and spry young buck,
        the dreamy swain if he's love-struck,
        the enraged one if he's jealous.

        He must recite his lines and play
        with so much skill and good sense too,
        that he transforms himself into
        the character he's to portray.

        His expert tongue of an artiste
        must give each line its full value,

---

*   This speech and Pedro's that follows have been transposed to allow Pedro a culminating speech about acting and to give the play a celebratory finale with Pedro addressing the whole company.

to bring to life and to renew
a tale of folk long since deceased.

He should shock with transformations,
turning tears to laughter and then
quickly make them return again
into mournful lamentations.

And if he sees his own expression
mirrored and equally intense
in faces in the audience,
he's at the top of his profession.

Enter PLAYER 3.

PLAYER 3: Hurry, their Majesties await
      they want to begin the play.
PEDRO: Tell them that I'm on my way.
PLAYER 3: Come on, they're saying that you're late.

PEDRO: Ladies and Gentlemen the royal party
      is waiting in the Palace and I'm afraid
      that you lot can't go in to see the play
      that my director's putting on because
      guards with pikes and staves and muskets
      are making sure no common plebs get in.
      We'll perform again tomorrow in this theatre
      and for a fee even you lot can afford,
      you'll see this whole story from start to finish
      and it won't end in marriage, as you'll see,
      that's always such a cliché, don't you think?
      [Neither will you see in it a lady
      give birth in one act to a baby boy,
      who in the next act with a beard already,
      kills fiercely all who wronged his ma and pa
      and in the end comes to rule a kingdom
      in some uncharted imaginary region.
      Such incongruous implausibilities
      have no part in the play that I present.]

It's wrought with artifice and artful splendour
from the life of Pedro the Great Pretender.

The end of the play.

APPENDIX

The following songs have variant lyrics set by Ilona Sekacz for the RSC production.

Night of St John

MUSICIANS: *Girl on a balcony,*
girl behind bars,
the love you are waiting for,
stands just outside your door.

Oh night of St John.

(*Spoken.*) He who came before,
whose hands told the time
better than a clock's,

his saintly finger told
that the day was here,
when light came to the world
and night would fall no more;
(*Sung.*) reveal yourself to us,
and may the dawn pour
dewdrops that shine like pearls
upon every flower
and while you are waiting
for the rising sun,
tell my girl in tones
that no discord mars:

Girl on a balcony,
girl behind bars,
the love you are waiting for,,
stands just outside your door.

(*Spoken.*) Tell Benita 'tis she
that Pascual adores

he's shepherd to the love
that pastures in his heart.
Tell Clemency as well
that he who's her lord
is her most humble slave,
it's written in the stars;
(*Sung.*) and don't forget the girl
who starts to lose heart
in what she wishes for,
(*Spoken.*) take her hand in yours
and whisper to her low,
or raise your voice high
(*Sung.*) so that in her yearnings
she must hear your calls:

Girl on a balcony,
girl behind bars,
the love you are waiting for,
stands just outside your door.

CLEMENTE: (*Spoken.*) The singing of the song was good.
      Come let's put around this portal
      some of the branches we've supplied –
      what are you doing here Pascual,
      with these two others at you side?

      Help us here to woo Benita,
      we'll both serve and entreat her
      by putting branches round her door:
      even if affection's dying
      that will be revivifying.

      (*Sung.*) Let's put the laurel on this side
      and the willow on the other
      and place the white poplar here,
      and let gillyflower,
      and Jasmine appear.

Sedge will turn the ground to em'rald,
woad will turn it into topaz
In between let's festoon garlands
so that every space is filled.

BENITA: (*Spoken.*) Please let the music play again, Señores,

so Clemency may hear it too and you (*To PASCUAL.*)
my Rook,
She leaves the window.
must make it sound again.

PASCUAL: Alright,
sweet instrument of my confirmation.
(*Sung.*) The jingling tambourines shall sound once more,
the guitars shall be strummed and flourishes
be played again;

MUSICIANS: *let's solemnise this morn,*
let's solemnise this morn,
let's solemnise this morn,
let's solemnise this morn,
morn, morn, morn, morn, morn,

PASCUAL: (*for it's the wish of her, whom I revere*).

CLEMENTE: (*Spoken.*) Sing on, and then let's go, the day is near!

MUSICIANS: (*Sung.*) *The thorns and brambles placed*
in my sweet love's bower,
each one of them shall be
turned into a flower.
Oh night of St John

The ash with his rough bark
and the mighty oak,
when placed at the door
will see themselves become
sacred scented groves,
transformed by her glance
Where'er she rests her eyes,

123

or puts her gentle foot,
the grass grows green,
for her, the fields are gay,
she gladdens every heart,
And all men fall in love,
serfs fall for her charms,
and their lordships cower.
*Each one of them shall
become a flower*

for her, the fields are gay,
she gladdens every heart,
And all men fall in love,

for her, the fields are gay,
she gladdens every heart,
And all men fall in love.

Song of the PLAYERS overheard by the KING

PLAYERS: Dance gypsy, Dance.
It's time to start,
so dance for the King
to the beat of his heart.
The Queen whose jealousy's
torn her apart,
will send you to jail,
now you've danced on her heart.
Like the gifts from our lord,
which the three Magi brought.
Inés and Belica bring dancing to court
Dance gypsy, Dance.
Belica brings dancing to court.
Dance gypsy, Dance.

Belica is nervous,
but the King is entranced
and offers her his hand,
when she trips in the dance.
Dance gypsy, Dance.
Belica's so lovely that jealousy burns
in the heart of the Queen,
who tosses and turns,
controlling her feelings,
lest madness prevail.
She points at the gypsies and sends them to jail.

Like the gifts from our lord,
which the three Magi brought.
Inés and Belica bring dancing to court
Dance gypsy, Dance.
Belica brings dancing to court.
Dance gypsy, Dance.